W. (William) Chappell, H. Ellis (Harry Ellis) Wooldridge

**Old English Popular Music**

W. (William) Chappell, H. Ellis (Harry Ellis) Wooldridge
**Old English Popular Music**
ISBN/EAN: 9783744690171

Printed in Europe, USA, Canada, Australia, Japan

Cover: Foto ©Thomas Meinert / pixelio.de

More available books at **www.hansebooks.com**

# Old English Popular Music

BY

*WILLIAM CHAPPELL, F.S.A.*

A NEW EDITION

WITH A PREFACE AND NOTES, AND THE EARLIER

EXAMPLES ENTIRELY REVISED

BY

*H. ELLIS WOOLDRIDGE*

VOL. II.

LONDON
*CHAPPELL & CO.* AND *MACMILLAN & CO.*
NEW YORK
*NOVELLO, EWER & CO.*
1893

# EDITOR'S PREFACE.

HITHERTO, as we have seen, the English ballad and dance tunes have followed a course in many respects parallel to that of the contemporary skilled music. The same scales, the same modulations, and often the same phrases of melody, have been employed in both; and the popular music, allowance being made for its inherent simplicity of design, has been found in no way inferior to its learned companion. But, henceforward, the reader will not fail to remark that, though this parallel course cannot be said to be discontinued, in one important respect there is a great difference between the two kinds of music which before did not exist; for while the skilled composers, in pursuit of the new musical ideal, shew no abatement of energy, the characteristic of the popular tunes is a gradually increasing languor and poverty of invention.

This may perhaps be accounted for by the natural dependence of the popular upon the learned music. Before 1600 the popular composers derived instruction and support not only indirectly from the learned compositions in parts, but also directly from those which were made for a single voice; these latter being almost without exception written in metrical form, and in a robust and straightforward style of melody, proper to the modal system, and congenial to the popular taste. But at the period we are now entering upon, the skilled composers, here as well as abroad, were applying themselves to the development of music for the single voice in ways which were quite unsuitable to the popular necessities; and their compositions, even when they were thrown into metrical form, were generally marked by a character of elegance, foreign in its origin, and unsympathetic to the usual audience of the fiddler, the ballad-singer, and the convivial songster of the tavern. The popular writers of this period, therefore, between their technical superiors on the one hand, on whom they were obliged to lean, and their popular clients on the other, whom they were bound to satisfy, were placed in a difficulty unknown before; and it is probably this difficulty which to some extent paralysed their powers of invention, and drove them to imitations either of the learned music which they were unable to appreciate, or of the older popular music which was growing every day more and more out of date. Be the cause, however, what it may, abundant proof that one or other of these courses was generally taken will be found in the following pages; and if the result, brilliant exceptions notwithstanding, is a general weakness and, compared with earlier examples, almost a sense of failure, it is because neither alternative offered much chance of success.

---

THE sources from which the tunes in the present volume have been taken are all, with a few unimportant exceptions, printed collections of the most popular songs and dance tunes in vogue at the date of publication. The earliest of these, Playford's great repertory, *The Dancing Master*, has been already described in the preface to the first volume; the most considerable of the remainder here follow:—

1. "Musick's Recreation on the Lyra Viol. Being a choice Collection of New and Excellent Lessons for the Lyra Viol, both easie and delightfull for all yong Practitioners. . . . . London, printed for John Playford, and are to be sold at his shop in the Inner Temple. 1653."

2. "Musick's Delight on the Cithren, Restored and Refined to a more easie and Pleasant Manner of Playing than formerly; And set forth with Lessons *A la Mode*, being the Choicest of our late new *Ayres Corants, Sarabands, Tunes*, and *Jiggs*. . . . . By John Playford Philo-Musicæ. London, Printed by W. G. and are sold by J. Playford at his shop in the Temple. 1666."

Notwithstanding this title, the work contains a large number of tunes much older than the date of the book itself, which when they can be compared so closely correspond with quite early versions, that even where comparison was not possible I considered myself justified in adopting them for songs in the first volume, if no earlier copy could be found.

3. "Choice Ayres, Songs, & Dialogues to sing to the Theorbo-lute, or Bass-viol. .... 1676."

This is another of Playford's publications, a reprint, with large additions, of a work which had appeared first in 1673, and again in 1675, entitled *Choice Songs and Ayres for One Voyce*, &c. A second volume was published in 1679, a third in 1681, a fourth in 1683, and a fifth in 1684.

4. "Wit and Mirth: or Pills to purge Melancholy; being a collection of the best Merry Ballads and Songs, Old and New. Fitted to all Humours, having each their proper Tune for either Voice or Instrument, many of the Songs being new Set. .... London, Printed by Will. Pearson, for Henry Playford, at his shop in the Temple-Change. 1699." A second part, "with several New Songs by Mr. D'Urfey; also, an Addition of Excellent Poems," appeared in the following year.

It would seem that a second edition, enlarged to four volumes, was published in 1707-9, and a third, in five volumes, in 1712-14. In 1719 appeared another, also in five volumes, with the title unaltered, (except that it now bears the name of J. Tonson as publisher,) but the contents edited and re-arranged by T. D'Urfey: a sixth volume followed in the next year. This work like *Musick's Delight*, contains a large number of tunes older than the date of the book, but generally much corrupted.

5. "The Merry Musician; or, a Cure for the Spleen: being a collection of the most diverting Songs and pleasant Ballads, set to Musick. .... London, printed by H. Meere, for J. Walsh. .... 1716." Vol. 2 appeared in 1728, vol. 3 in 1731, and vol. 4 in 1733.

6. "The Compleat Country Dancing-Master: containing great variety of Dances, both Old and New. .... London, Printed by H. Meere, for J. Walsh. .... 1718." A second part appeared in the next year, and several editions followed.

7. "The Musical Miscellany; being a Collection of Choice Songs, set to the Violin and Flute, by the most Eminent Masters. .... London, Printed by and for John Watts, at the Printing-Office in Wild-Court, near Lincoln's-Inn-Fields." Vols. 1 and 2 appeared in 1729, vols. 3 and 4 in 1730, and vols. 5 and 6 in 1731.

From this time onward books of dance tunes, such as Thompson's *Choice Collection of* 200, &c., continued to be published as before, but the collections of songs were now almost entirely superseded by the Ballad Operas, which appeared henceforward in large numbers until the close of the period with which the present work has to do. The first of these productions was the *Beggar's Opera*, given in 1728, and its feigned purpose, which the spectators are informed was originally to grace the wedding of a beggar and a ballad singer, supplied a natural occasion for the employment of ballad tunes throughout. These were printed with the words at the date of the performance, and a more expensive edition of the book, with basses by Dr. Pepusch set to the tunes, came out in the following year. The enormous popularity of this opera established the ballad form, and it continued to be used without apology, for every kind of subject, during many years. Of the ballad operas which were printed the most important for the purposes of this work are the following :—

The Quaker's Opera, 1728.
Polly, 1729.
The Village Opera, 1729.
Love in a Riddle, 1729.
The Cobbler's Opera, 1729.
The Patron, &c., 1729.
Momus turned Fabulist, 1729.
Flora, 1729.
The Lover's Opera, 1729.
The Bays' Opera, 1730.
Robin Hood, 1730.

The Fashionable Lady, 1730.
The Jovial Crew, 1731.
Silvia, 1731.
The Grub Street Opera, 1731.
Humours of the Court, 1732.
The Stage Mutineers, 1733.
Achilles, 1733.
The Boarding School, 1733.
The Livery Rake, 1733.
The Devil to pay, 1748.
Love in a Village, 1762.

I cannot conclude my remarks upon the present edition without a word of regret for the exclusion of the tunes which rest upon no better authority than tradition. Many of these tunes, given in the work of 1855, have deservedly become established favourites with the public, and I am quite prepared to find their absence deplored by not a few of my readers. But I must urge that in coming to a decision upon them the question of their intrinsic merit was not for me to consider. I could only have regard to the plain rule that a tune which rests upon oral tradition alone has no proper place in a work based in principle upon documentary evidence. Our author, it is true, took a different view of the possibilities of the case; but at the time when his editions were published so little had as yet been done to rescue any of the old popular music from oblivion that he must be held fully justified in deciding as he did.

Since then, however, several excellent collections of the tunes which depend upon oral tradition alone have been made, and the time has now come, in my opinion, when this work may with advantage be restricted within its own proper limits. Traditional tunes are, from their nature, of especially obscure origin and uncertain date ; they can seldom, indeed, be effectually traced beyond the singer from whose mouth they are taken down. To gather them into collections confined to their own class of music, where they appear in their true character and rest upon their intrinsic merit, is to do them most justice; to include them in a work like the present, where they are associated with proved early versions of old tunes, is to lend them the appearance of an authority which they cannot possess, and which moreover they do not need to recommend them.

LONDON,
*September*, 1893.

# TABLE OF TUNES

CONTAINED IN THE

## SECOND VOLUME.

THE LATER SONGS, BALLADS, AND DANCE TUNES.

| | PAGE | | PAGE |
|---|---|---|---|
| The Buff Coat has no fellow | 1 | The twenty-ninth of May | 52 |
| Jamaica | 3 | Oh how they frisk it, or Leather apron, or Under the greenwood tree | 53 |
| Law lies a-bleeding, or The Dominion of the Sword | 5 | | |
| London is a fine town, or Watton town's end | 6 | Mad Robin | 56 |
| | | Joan's placket is torn | 57 |
| The New Royal Exchange | 8 | Lilliburlero | 58 |
| Waits' Music | 10 | The King of Poland, or Courtiers, courtiers | 60 |
| Amarillis | 12 | |  |
| I am a poor shepherd undone, or Hey, ho, my honey | 14 | I often for my Jenny strove | 61 |
| | | The Rant | 63 |
| The blind beggar of Bethnal Green | 16 | Ladies of London | 64 |
| Thomas, you cannot | 17 | James the Second's March, or The Garter | 65 |
| Here's a health unto his Majesty | 18 | | |
| Franklin is fled away | 20 | The Northumberland bagpipes | 66 |
| The Northern lass | 21 | Willy was so blithe a lad | 68 |
| Bonny Nell | 23 | The baffled Knight | 69 |
| The lass of Cumberland | 24 | Aye, marry, and thank ye too | 70 |
| Cavalilly man | 26 | Red Bull | 71 |
| The fit's upon me now | 27 | Greenwich Park, or Come, sweet lass | 73 |
| The delights of the bottle | 28 | Mad Moll, or The virgin queen, or Yellow stockings | 74 |
| In January last | 30 | | |
| The clear Cavalier | 32 | The Devil's progress | 75 |
| The fair one let me in | 34 | Bartholomew Fair, or The Dutchwoman's Jigg | 77 |
| Young Jemmy | 36 | | |
| When busy Fame | 39 | Tobacco's but an Indian weed | 78 |
| Cock Lorrel | 40 | There was an old woman liv'd under a hill | 79 |
| A begging we will go | 42 | | |
| I'll tell thee, Dick, where I have been | 43 | The Cobbler's Hornpipe | 80 |
| Roger of Coverly | 45 | Lay the bent to the bonny broom | 80 |
| When the stormy winds do blow | 47 | An old woman poor and blind | 82 |
| The King's Jig, or At Winchester was a wedding | 49 | Shackley-Hay | 83 |
| | | The Spanish lady | 84 |

|                                                    | PAGE |                                                     | PAGE |
| -------------------------------------------------- | ---- | --------------------------------------------------- | ---- |
| I have but a mark a year                           |  86  | The leather bottle                                  | 141  |
| Old Noll's Jig                                     |  87  | Sweet William's farewell to black-ey'd Susan        | 144  |
| Portsmouth                                         |  88  | All in the Downs                                    | 145  |
| Turn again, Whittington                            |  89  | Come, open the door, sweet Betty                    | 147  |
| Felton's Gavot, or Farewell, Manchester            |  91  | Cupid's Trepan                                      | 149  |
| Admiral Benbow                                     |  92  | The doubting virgin, or Woman's work is never done  | 150  |
| Benbow, the brother tar                            |  94  | The Oxfordshire tragedy                             | 153  |
| The roast beef of old England                      |  95  | To all you ladies now at land                       | 154  |
| Three travellers                                   |  97  | Sir Guy                                             | 156  |
| Good morrow, gossip Joan                           |  98  | There was an old fellow at Waltham Cross, or Taunton Dean | 158 |
| Cupid's courtesie, or I am so deep in love         |  96  | The bailiff's daughter                              | 159  |
| Joan to the maypole                                | 100  | There lives a lass upon the green                   | 160  |
| St. George for England                             | 102  | Three merry men of Kent                             | 161  |
| The fading                                         | 104  | Lovely Nancy                                        | 162  |
| Come let us prepare                                | 105  | Old Hewson the cobbler                              | 163  |
| Here's a health to all honest men                  | 107  | The sailor's complaint                              | 165  |
| The happy clown                                    | 108  | The dusty miller                                    | 166  |
| Come, jolly Bacchus, or Charles of Sweden          | 109  | Cheshire Rounds                                     | 167  |
| The mousetrap, or Old Hob                          | 111  | Shropshire Rounds                                   | 168  |
| The man of Kent                                    | 112  | There was a pretty lass and a tenant of my own      | 169  |
| May Fair                                           | 113  | Death and the lady                                  | 170  |
| Come lasses and lads                               | 114  | Old King Cole                                       | 171  |
| Poor Robin's maggot                                | 116  | Down among the dead men                             | 173  |
| Sally in our alley                                 | 117  | A-hunting we will go                                | 175  |
| Cease your funning                                 | 119  | Humours of the bath, or The spring's a-coming       | 177  |
| An old woman clothed in gray                       | 120  | Molly's hoop                                        | 178  |
| The country garden, or The Vicar of Bray           | 122  | O good ale, thou art my darling                     | 179  |
| The Budgeon it is a delicate trade                 | 124  | Come, let us drink about                            | 180  |
| Sweet Nelly, my heart's delight                    | 125  | Pretty Polly Oliver                                 | 181  |
| As down in the meadows                             | 127  | The women all tell me                               | 182  |
| The country courtship                              | 128  | The Barking barber                                  | 183  |
| Grim King of the Ghosts                            | 129  | Care, thou canker of our joys                       | 184  |
| Fair Rosalind                                      | 131  | Smiling Polly, or The keel row                      | 185  |
| Fair Margaret and sweet William                    | 131  | Nancy Dawson, or Miss Dawson's Hornpipe             | 186  |
| Phillida flouts me                                 | 133  | Brighton Camp, or The girl I've left behind me      | 187  |
| The Duke of Berwick's March, or Why, soldiers, why? or How stands the glass around? | 134 | Heart of Oak | 189 |
| On yonder high mountains                           | 136  | Rule, Britannia                                     | 191  |
| On the cold ground, or I prethee, love, turn to me | 137  | God save our lord the King                          | 194  |
| My lodging it is on the cold ground                | 140  |                                                     |      |

# THE LATER POPULAR MUSIC.

## SONGS, BALLADS, AND DANCE TUNES.

---

### THE BUFF COAT HAS NO FELLOW.

*The Dancing Master*, 4th and all subsequent editions: in the later editions with the name of "Excuse me." Ballad operas.

In Fletcher's play, *The Knight of Malta*, act iii., sc. 1, there is a "Song by the Watch," commencing thus :—

> "Sit, soldiers, sit and sing, the *Round* is clear,
> And cock-a-loodle-loo tells us the day is near ;
> Each toss his can until his throat be mellow,
> Drink, laugh, and sing *The soldier has no fellow*."

The last line is repeated in three out of the four verses or parts, and I suppose *The soldier has no fellow* to have been then a well-known song.

As various ballads were written to the tune called *The buff coat has no fellow* (see, for instance, Pepys Coll., iii. 150 ; Roxburghe, i. 536, &c.), and as the buff coat was a distinguishing mark of the soldier of the seventeenth century, the latter song, if the words could be recovered, might prove to be the one I suppose to have been referred to by Fletcher.

The following list of ballad-operas, in all of which songs may be found written to the tune, sufficiently proves its former popularity :—*Polly* ; *The Lottery* ; *An Old Man taught Wisdom* ; *The Intriguing Chambermaid* ; *The Lover's Opera* ; *The Bay's Opera* ; *The Lover his own Rival* ; *The Grub Street Opera* ; *The Devil of a Duke, or Trapolin's Vagaries* ; *The Fashionable Lady, or Harlequin's Opera* ; *The Generous Freemason* ; and *The Footman*.

This popularity extended to Ireland and Scotland ; and although, in its old form, purely English in character, the air has been claimed both as Irish and as Scotch. T. Moore appropriated it, under the name of *My husband's a journey to Portugal gone*, and it has been claimed in Scotland as *The Deuks dang o'er my Daddie*.

In some copies of *The Dancing Master* the tune is in common time, and in several of the ballad-operas, whether under the name of *Buff coat*, or *Excuse me* (see, for instance, *The Generous Freemason*, 1731), it commences thus :—

Other changes for the worse were also made in the tune before the use of it was given up.

## JAMAICA.

*The Dancing Master*, 4th edition, and all after.

This tune appeared shortly after the taking of Jamaica from the Spaniards in 1655, and probably took its name from some song on that event, now lost.

The following were sung to it :—

1. "The Prodigal's Resolution ; or, My Father was born before me" (*Pills to purge Melancholy*, vol. i., 1699 and 1707). This is taken from

Thomas Jordan's *London Triumphant*, 4to. 1672. Jordan was the "professed pageant-writer and poet laureate for the City, and if author of this song," says Ritson, who includes it in his *Ancient Songs*, "he seems to have possessed a greater share of poetical merit than usually fell to the lot of his profession." It begins with the line, "I am a lusty, lively lad," which was probably suggested by, and the tune taken from, an earlier song, beginning—

"Heigh for a lusty, lively lad," &c.

to be found in a medley of songs at p. 30 of *Sportive Wit: The Muses' Merriment*, 8vo, 1656.

2. "Two Toms and Nat in council sat. To the tune of *Jamaica*." (*State Poems, continued*, p. 140, 1697.)

4. "Slow men of London; or, The Widow Brown" (*Pills*, vi. 93). This is a song of three Londoners being outwitted by a Welshman, in a competition for the Widow Brown. It consists of twelve stanzas, and commences thus :—

"There dwelt a widow in this town
That was both fair and lovely;

* * * * * * *

There were three young men of this town,
Slow men from London,
And they'd go woo the Widow Brown,
Because they would be undone."

The last four lines form the subject of another song, which is printed in Watts' *Musical Miscellany*, ii. 74, 1729. It consists of only sixteen lines, and is said to have been sung in the play of *Wit without Money;* I suppose on the revival of Beaumont and Fletcher's play, about the year 1708, with alterations and, as the title-page modestly asserts, "with *amendments*, by some persons of quality." It suggests the possibility of the longer song having been introduced in 1639 or 1661. There is a situation for one near the end of the play, but (according to the Rev. A. Dyce) it is not printed either in the quartos or in the folio.

Three other songs are printed to the tune in *Pills to purge Melancholy*, viz., "The Angler's Song," beginning, "Of all the recreations" (iii. 126); "Of the Downfall of one part of the Mitre Tavern in Cambridge, or the sinking thereof into the cellar" (iii. 136); and "The Jolly Tradesmen," beginning, "Some time I am a tapster new" (vi. 91). Others will be found in the ballad-operas of *Polly*, 1829; *Love and Revenge*, n.d., &c.

## LAW LIES A-BLEEDING, or THE DOMINION OF THE SWORD.

*The Dancing Master*, 1665, there called "Dove's Catastrophe, or Lawyers your pleading"; also in editions of 1686, &c.; *Loyal Songs*, 1685, &c.; Walsh's *Dancing Master*; *Pills to purge Melancholy*, &c.

In *The Loyal Garland*, 5th edition, 1686, is "The Dominion of the Sword: A Song made in the Rebellion." Commencing :—

"Lay by your pleading, Law lies a-bleeding,
 Burn all your studies, and throw away your reading," &c.

It is also in *Loyal Songs*, i. 223, 1731 (there entitled "The *Power* of the Sword"); in *Merry Drollery Complete*, 1661 and 1670; in *Pills to purge Melancholy*, vi. 190, &c.

In Shadwell's *Epsom Wells*, 1673, Clodpate sings, "the old song, *Lay by your pleading, Law lies a-bleeding.*"

"A new Ignoramus: Being the second new song to the same old tune, *Law lies a-bleeding*," was printed by Charles Leigh in 1681, and included in *Rome rhym'd to death*, 8vo, 1683. It commences :—

"Since Popish plotters joined with bog-trotters,
 Sham plots are made as fast as pots are form'd by potters."

This is included in 180 *Loyal Songs*, 1685 and 1694, with several other political songs to the same tune.

"*Love lies a-bleeding*; in imitation of *Law lies a-bleeding*," is contained in *Merry Drollery Complete*, 1661 and 1670. There are also copies in ballad form, in which the tune is entitled *The Cyclops*; it begins :—

"Lay by your pleading, Love lies a-bleeding,
 Burn all your poetry, and throw away your reading."

The ballad is political, but there was perhaps an older song with the same name. *Love lyes a-bleeding* is the second title of Beaumont and Fletcher's play of *Philaster*, 1620; and Whitelock (*Zootomia, or Present Manners of the English*, 1654) says "Both truth and love lie a-bleeding."

In the Bagford Collection, a song, "printed at the Hague, for S. Browne, 1659," is named "Chips of the Old Block; or, Hercules cleansing the Augean Stable. To the tune of *The Sword.*" It commences:—

"Now you, by your good leave, sirs, shall see the Rump can cleave, sirs,
And what chips from this treacherous block will come, you may conceive, sirs."

Other copies of this will be found in King's Pamphlets, vol. xvi.; in *Rats rhymed to death*, 1660; and in *Loyal Songs*, ii. 53.

## LONDON IS A FINE TOWN, OR WATTON TOWN'S END.

*The Dancing Master*, 1665, &c.; *Pills to purge Melancholy*, 1707; *The Beggars' Opera.*

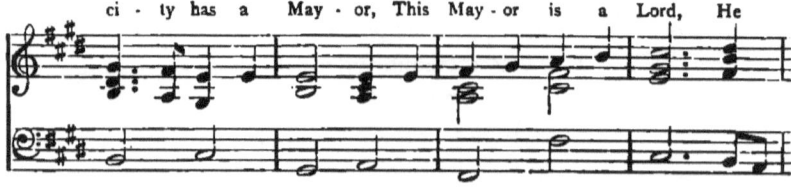

The original song, "Oh! London is a fine town," is probably no longer extant; the words given above are taken from a song in *Pills to purge Melancholy*, ii. 40, 1707, or iv. 40, 1719. Another, very like it, is in *Le Prince d'Amour*, 12mo, 1660; it begins thus:—

> " London is a fine town, and a brave city,
> Governed with scarlet gowns; give ear unto my ditty:
> And there is a Mayor, which Mayor he is a Lord,
> That governeth the city by righteous record."

Another will be found in the King's Pamphlets, British Museum (fol. broadsides, vol. v.). It begins, " Why kept your train-bands such a stir," and is dated August 13, 1647. (Reprinted in Wright's *Political Ballads* for the Percy Society.)

A ballad to be sung to the tune was written on the occasion of James I.'s visit to Cambridge, in March, 1614:—

> " Cambridge is a merry town,
> And Oxford is another," &c.

This will be found in Nichols' *Progresses of King James*, vol. ii., p. 73.

In *The Dancing Master* the tune is called *Watton Town's End*, from a ballad of that name, beginning:—

> " As I came from Arpenden,
> and straight to Watton Town," &c.

Another, to be found in the same volume as the words printed with the tune, begins:—

> " As I came from Tottingham,
> upon a market day," &c.

And in the same collection (1707, iii. 219, or 1719, v. 139) there is a song called " Bonny Peggy Ramsey," to the same tune.

One of D'Urfey's " Scotch" Songs, called " The Gowlin," in his play of *Trick for Trick*, was also sung to this tune.

*The Button'd Smock* is another name for the tune (see *Pills to purge Melancholy*, 1719, vol. vi., p. 145); and in the Pepys Collection, i. 406, is " The Cuckowes Comendation, &c. Being a merry Maying Song in praise of the Cuckow. To the tune of *The Button'd Smocke*. Pr. for M. R." It begins:—

> " Of all the birds that haunts the woods."

## THE NEW ROYAL EXCHANGE.

*The Dancing Master*, 1665, &c.

In *Wit and Drollery*, 1656, p. 110, is a song to this tune—" On the Souldiers walking in the New Exchange to affront the Ladies." It begins :—

> " I'll go no more to the New Exchange,
> There is no room at all," &c.

In the same book, at p. 60, is another song of six stanzas, beginning :—

> " We'll go no more to Tunbridge Wells,
> The journey is too far," &c.

In *Westminster Drollery*, part ii., 1671, is a third song, " to tune of *I'll go no more to the New Exchange;* " beginning :—

> " Never will I wed a girl that's coy,
> Nor one that is too free," &c.

In *Wit Restored, in severall select Poems, not formerly publisht*, 1658, there are two songs, " The Burse of Reformation,"[1] and " The Answer." The first commencing :—

> " We will go no more to the Old Exchange,
> There's no good ware at all ;
> Their bodkins, and their thimbles, too,
> Went long since to Guildhall.
> But we will go to the New Exchange,
> Where all things are in fashion," &c.

And " The Answer " :—

> " We will go no more to the New Exchange,
> Their credit's like to fall,
> Their money and their loyalty
> Is gone to Goldsmiths' Hall.[2]
> But we will keep our Old Exchange,
> Where wealth is still in fashion," &c.

These have been reprinted in *Satirical Songs and Poems on Costume*, for the Percy Society, by F. W. Fairholt, F.S.A.

" The New Exchange," in *Merry Drollery Complete*, 1670, p. 134, commencing :—

> " I'll go no more to the Old Exchange,
> There's no good ware at all ;
> But I will go to the New Exchange,
> Call'd Haberdashers' Hall :
> For there are choice of knacks and toys,
> The fancy for to please."

---

[1] King James I. named the New Exchange " Britain's Burse."

[2] The place appointed for the reception of fines imposed upon the Royalists; and for loans, &c., to the Puritanic party.

## WAITS' MUSIC.

The musicians of towns and corporations were called Waits[1]; and it would appear that the waits of each town had some special tune to which they gave their name. Many of these tunes have been preserved; as the *Worksop Waits*, in the B.M. MSS.; *York Waits*, printed in broadsides; *Bristol Waits*, in *Apollo's Banquet*; *Warrington Waits*, in Walsh's *Dancing Master*, &c. A few specimens here follow:—

### LONDON WAITS.

*The Dancing Master*, 1665; *Apollo's Banquet*, 1669.

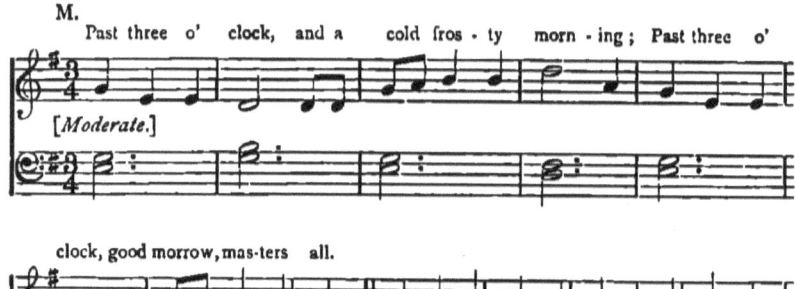

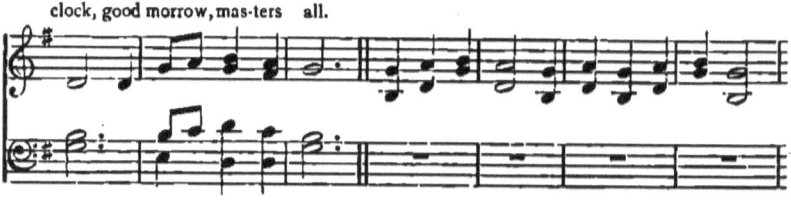

---

[1] In nearly all the books of household expenditure in early times we find donations to waits of the towns through which the traveller passed. In those of Sir John Howard, of Henry VII., and of Henry VIII., there are payments to the waits of London, Colchester, Dover, Canterbury, Dartford, Coventry, Northampton, and others. Will. Kemp, in his celebrated Morris-dance from London to Norwich, says that few cities have waits like those of Norwich, and none better; and that, besides their excellency in wind instruments, their rare cunning on the viol and violin, they had admirable voices, every one of them being able to serve as a chorister in any cathedral church. Waits, or Waights, seem to have been originally watchmen, who, to prove their watchfulness, were required to pipe at stated hours of the night. Among the servants in Edward IV.'s household the *Liber Niger Domus Regis* includes "A Wayte, that nightely from Mychelmas to Shreve Thorsdaye *pipethe watche* within this courte fowere tymes; in the Somere nightes three tymes, and makethe *bon gayte* at every chambere doare and offyce, as well for feare of pyckeres and pillers. He eatethe in the halle with Mynstrelles, and takethe lyverey at nighte a loafe, a galone of ale, and for Somere nightes two candles [of] pich, and a bushel of coles; and for Wintere nightes halfe a loafe of bread, a galone of ale, four candles pich, a bushel coles, &c. . . . . Also this Yeoman-Waighte, at the making of Knightes of the Bathe, for his attendance upon them by nightetime, in watchinge in the Chappelle, hathe to his fee all the watchinge clothing that the Knight shall wear upon him."

THE LATER POPULAR MUSIC. 11

The livery of the London Waits in 1575 is described (in Fairholt's *Lord Mayor's Pageants*, pt. 1, p. 23) as "blue gowns, red sleeves and caps, every one having his silver collar about his neck."

In 1599, Morley thus speaks of them in his dedication of his *Consort Lessons*, for six instruments, to the Lord Mayor and Aldermen :—" But, as the ancient custom of this most honourable and renowned city hath been ever to retain and maintain excellent and expert musicians, to adorn your Honour's favours, feasts, and solemn meetings,—to those, your Lordship's Wayts, I recommend the same,—to your servants' careful and skilful handling."

When Charles II., on his restoration, passed through the city of London to Whitehall, he was, according to Ogilby, entertained with music from a band of eight waits at Crutched Friars, of six at Aldgate, and six in Leadenhall Street.

CHESTER WAITS.

Walsh's *Compleat Country Dancing Master*, iii. 36.

### COLCHESTER WAITS.

*Apollo's Banquet*, 1669.

### AMARILLIS.

*The Dancing Master*, 1665; *Musick's Delight on the Cithren*, 1666; *Apollo's Banquet*, 1670, &c

1. A - ma - ril - lis told her swain, A - ma - ril - lis told her swain,

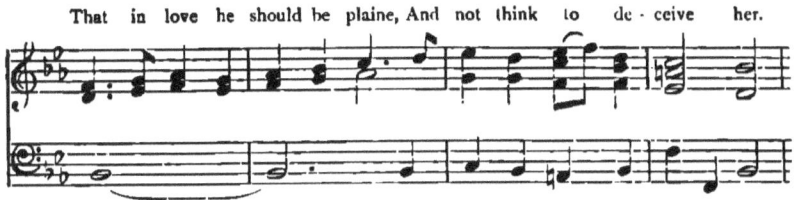

If thou dost keep thy vow, quoth she,
If thou dost keep thy vow, quoth she,
There's never a swain in all this Plain,
That ever shall come near thee,
  For Garlands and Embroidered Scrips
  For I do love thee dearly.

But Colin, if thou change thy love,
But Colin, if thou change thy love,
A Tigris then I'le to the prove,
If ere thou dost come near me.
  Amarillis fear not that,
  For I do love thee dearly.

The song of "Amarillis" is in Porter's play *The Villain*, 1663; also printed in *Merry Drollery Complete*, 1670, and in *The New Academy of Compliments*.

The air is sometimes referred to as *Phillis on the new-made hay*, from a ballad entitled "The Coy Shepherdess; or Phillis and Amintas"; which was sung to the tune of *Amarillis.*—(See Roxburghe Collection, ii. 85.)

Among the ballads to the air are also the following:—

"The Royal Recreation of Jovial Anglers," beginning—

    "Of all the recreations which
    Attend on human nature," &c.
                  *Roxburghe Collection;*

Collier's Roxburghe Ballads, p. 232; and *Merry Drollery Complete*, 1661 and 1670. It is also in *Pills to purge Melancholy;* but there set to the tune of *My father was born before me*.

"Love in the blossom; or Fancy in the bud: to the tune *Amarillis told her swain.*"—(Roxburghe, ii. 315.)

"Fancy's Freedom; or true Lovers' bliss: tune of *Amarillis*, or *Phillis on the new-made hay.*"—(Roxburghe, iii. 114.)

"The True Lovers' Happiness; or Nothing venture, nothing have,"
&c.: tune of *Amintas on the new-made hay;* or *The Loyal Lovers."*
—(Douce Collection, and Roxburghe, ii. 486.)

"The Cotsall [Cotswold] Shepherds: to the tune of *Amarillis told her swain,"* in *Folly in Print, or a Book of Rhymes,* 1667.

"The Virgin's Constancy; or The faithful Marriner: to the tune of *Amarillis";* and "The True Lovers' Happiness; or Nothing venture, nothing have: to the tune of *Amintas on the new-made hay";* both in the Pepys Collection, vol. iv., pp. 55 and 57.

## I AM A POOR SHEPHERD UNDONE,

### OR

### HEY, HO, MY HONEY!

*The Dancing Master,* 1665, 1686, and all subsequent editions; *Apollo's Banquet for the Treble Violin; Pills to purge Melancholy,* vi. 284, with the first name; *The Beggars' Opera,* &c.

## THE LATER POPULAR MUSIC.

If to love me she would not incline,
    I said I should die in an hour ;
"'To die," said she, "is in thine,
    But to love you is not in my power."
I ask'd her the reason why
    She could not of me approve ;
She said 'twas a task too hard,
    To give any reason for love.
        *And alas! poor Shepherd,* &c.

She asked me of my estate,
    I told her a flock of sheep ;
The grass whereon they graze,
    And where she and I might sleep :
Besides a good ten pound,
    In old King Harry's groats ;
While hooks and crooks abound,
    And birds of sundry notes.
        *And alas! poor Shepherd,* &c.

In the King's Pamphlets, vol. xv. fol. ; in the Bagford Collection, p. 67 ; in *Rump Songs*, 1662, part ii. p. 26 ; and in Wright's *Political Ballads*, p. 146, are copies of " A proper new Ballad on the Old Parliament, or the second part of Knave out of doores : to the tune of—

'Hei, ho, my honey, my heart shall never rue ;
Four-and-twenty now for your money, and yet a hard pennyworth too.' "

The copy in the King's Pamphlets is dated December 11, 1659. The ballad begins :—

"Good morrow, my neighbours all, what news is this I heard tell," &c.

In the Roxburghe Collection, ii. 54, and Collier's *Roxburghe Ballads*, p. 298, are "A Caveat for Young Men, or The bad husband turn'd thrifty," &c.  "To the tune of *Hey, ho, my honey!*" beginning, "All you young ranting blades that spend your time in vain," by John Wade. Printed by W. Thackeray, T. Passinger, and W. Whitwood.

*Hey, ho, my honey*, is also one of the tunes to which " The Valiant Seamen's Congratulation " to Charles II., on his accession, was to be sung.

## THE BLIND BEGGAR OF BETHNAL GREEN.

It was a blind beg-gar had long lost his sight, He

[*Moderate.*]

had a fair daugh-ter of beau-ty most bright, And ma-ny a gal-lant brave

sui-tor had she, For none was so come-ly as pret-ty Bes-sie.

This tune was found by Dr. Rimbault in a MS. volume of Lute Music written by Rogers, a celebrated lutenist of the reign of Charles II., in the library at Etwall Hall, Derbyshire. It is there called *The Cripple*, and the ballad of "The Stout Cripple of Cornwall" is directed to be sung to the tune of *The Blind Beggar.*—(See Roxburghe Collection, i. 389, and Bagford, i. 32). It is also in Evans' *Old Ballads*, i. 97, 1810.

"This popular old ballad," says Percy, "was written in the reign of Elizabeth, as appears not only from verse 23, where the arms of England are called the 'Queenes armes,' but from its tune being quoted in other old pieces written in her time. See the ballad on Mary Ambree," &c.

In a black-letter book called *The World's Folly*, we read that "a dapper fellow, that in his youth had spent more than he got, on his person, fell to singing 'The Blind Beggar,' to the tune of *Heigh ho !*"— (*Brit. Bibliographer*, ii. 560.)

In the *Collection of Loyal Songs written against the Rump Parliament*, and in *Rats rhimed to death, or the Rump Parliament hang'd up in the Shambles* (1660), are many songs to the tune of *The Blind Beggar*, as well as in the King's Pamphlets, Brit. Museum.

Among them, "A Hymn to the Gentle Craft, or Hewson's Lamentation" (a satire on Lord Hewson, one of Cromwell's lords, who had been a cobbler, and had but one eye), and "The Second Martyrdom of the Rump."

Pepys, in his diary, 25th June, 1663, speaks of going with Sir William and Lady Batten, and Sir J. Minnes, to Sir W. Rider's, at Bednall Green, to dinner, "a fine place;" and adds, "This very house was built by the blind Beggar of Bednall Green, so much talked of and sang in ballads; but they say it was only some outhouses of it." The house was called Kirby Castle.

The tune was sometimes called *Pretty Bessie*, and a ballad to be sung to it, under that name, is in the Roxburghe Collection, i. 142.

## THOMAS, YOU CANNOT.

*Musick's Delight on the Cithren*, 1666; *The Dancing Master*, 4th and later editions; Sir John Hawkins' transcripts; *The Beggars' Opera*, and many others.

The song of "Thomas, you cannot" is in Dr. Percy's folio MS. The name "Thomas, I cannot" is often given to the tune, referring probably to some song now lost. The tune itself, when it is for dancing, sometimes appears with eight bars, instead of ten, in the second part.

In the Pepys Collection, i. 62, is a black-letter ballad (one of the many written against the Roman Catholics after the discovery of the Gunpowder Plot, in 1605), entitled "A New-yeeres-Gift for the Pope; O come see the difference plainly decided between Truth and Falsehood:

"Not all the Pope's trinkets, which here are brought forth,
Can balance the bible, for weight or for worth," &c.

"To the tune of *Thomas, you cannot*." It commences thus:—

"All you that desirous are to behold
The difference 'twixt falsehood and faith," &c.

In *Grammatical Drollery, by W. H.* (Captain Hicks), 1682, p. 75, is a song commencing, "Come, my Molly, let us be jolly:" to the tune of *Thomas, I cannot*; and in Chetwood's *History of the Stage*, 8vo, 1749, a song on a theatrical anecdote, by Mr. John Leigh (an actor, who died in 1726).

## HERE'S A HEALTH UNTO HIS MAJESTY.

Playford's *Musical Companion*, 1667, 1672, &c.

## THE LATER POPULAR MUSIC.

This was a very popular loyal song in the reign of Charles II. It is twice mentioned by Shadwell in his plays. Firstly, in *The Miser* (1672), where Timothy says, "We can be merry as the best of you—we can, i' faith—and sing *A boat, a boat* [*Haste to the ferry*], or *Here's a health to his Majesty, with a fa, la, la, lero ;* " and secondly, in his *Epsom Wells* (1673), where Bisket says, "Come, let's all be musitioners, and all roar and sing *Here's a health unto his Majesty, with a fa, la, la, la, la, lero.*"

In *The Musical Companion* it appears as a three-part song, by Jeremiah Savile.

## FRANKLIN IS FLED AWAY.

*Apollo's Banquet for the Treble Violin*, 1669 ; *Loyal Songs*, 1685 and 1694 ;
*Pills to purge Melancholy*, iii. 208, 1707.

Franklin is fled and gone, O hone, O hone !
And left me here alone, O hone, O hone !
    Franklin is fled away,
    The glory of the May ;
Who can but mourn and say, O hone, O hone ! &c.

The title of this ballad is "A Mournful Caral ; or, An Elegy lamenting the tragical ends of two unfortunate faithful Lovers, Franklin and Cordelius; he being slain, she slew herself with her dagger. To a new tune called *Franklin is fled away*."

Copies are in the Pepys Collection, ii. 76 ; the Roxburghe, ii. 348 ; the Bagford, 643, m. 10, p. 69 ; and the Douce, fol. 222.

In the same volume of the Bagford Collection, p. 139, is "The Two Faithful Lovers. To the tune of *Franklin is fled away;*" commencing:—

> "Farewell, my heart's delight,
> Ladies, adieu !
> I must now take my flight,
> Whate'er ensue."

The tune is mentioned sometimes under the name of *Franklin is fled away,* and at others as *O hone, O hone,* the burden of the ballad. This burden is derived from the Irish lamentation, to which there were many allusions in the sixteenth and seventeenth centuries, as in Marston's *Eastward Hoe,* act v., sc. 1 ; or in Gayton's *Festivous Notes upon Don Quixote,* 1654, p. 57 : "Who this night is to be rail'd upon by the black-skins, in as lamentable noyse as the wild Irish make their *O hones.*" A different version of the tune will be found in the ballad opera of *The Jovial Crew,* 1731, under the name of *You gallant ladies all.*

A variety of songs and ballads, which were sung to it, will be found in the above-named collections of ballads ; in the 180 *Loyal Songs;* in Patrick Carey's *Trivial Poems,* 1651 ; and in *Pills to purge Melancholy.*

The tune is one of the many from which *God save the King* has been said to be derived.

## THE NORTHERN LASS.

*Apollo's Banquet,* 1669 ; *The Pleasant Companion, or New Instructions for the Flageolet,* by Thomas Greeting, gent., 1680. Also in *Pills to purge Melancholy;* Walsh's *New Country Dances,* 1713 ; Wright's *Country Dances; The Merry Musician;* and several ballad operas, much altered.

This is the version contained in *Apollo's Banquet;* the later one (which omits bars 12-19, inclusive) is more suitable to the ballad. The ballad is to be found in Roxburghe, ii. 161, and is there called "The Fickle Northern Lass, or the Wrong'd Shepherd's Resolution," &c. Tune of *There was a lass in the North Country.* It begins:—

> "There was a lass in the North Country,
> And she had lovers two or three:
> But she unkindly dealt by one,
> Who had to her great favour shewn.
> Which made him thus for to complain—
> I never shall see my love again,
> For since that she has chang'd her mind,
> I'll trust no more to womankind."

In Walsh's *Country Dances,* and in the ballad operas generally, the tune is called *Lord Frog,* from a song written to it by D'Urfey, beginning, "Great Lord Frog to Lady Mouse," &c. (see *Pills,* &c., 1719, vol. i., p. 14, and *Silvia,* p. 35); in Wright's *Country Dances* it is called *Muirland Willie.* In Shield's opera, *The Farmer,* it also appears, set to the song, "Look, dear Ma'am, I'm quite the thing."

The tune was published in 1830, under the title of "An old English air, arranged as a Rondo by Samuel Wesley"; but in his arrangement the later versions have been followed rather than the early one given above.

## BONNY NELL.

*Apollo's Banquet for the Treble Violin* (title page of copy wanting, probably edition of 1670).

This tune was probably originally a ballad tune, and different in some respects from the dance tune given above; for Dr. Corbet, afterwards Bishop of Norwich, wrote some verses to the tune of *Bonny Nell* which could not very well be sung to this air. They will be found in Nicholls' *Progresses of King James*, iii. 66.

The ballad, now lost, is mentioned in *The Anatomie of the English Nunnery at Lisbon*, published "by authoritie in 1622"; it seems to have been a favourite with the nuns of that convent.

Massinger alludes to some "Bonny Nell" in his *Old Law*, act iv., sc. 1, where the Cook says, "That Nell was Helen of Greece too"; and Gnotho answers, "As long as she tarried with her husband, she was

Ellen; but after she came to Troy, she was Nell of Troy, or Bonny Nell."

In the Pepys Collection, i. 70, is "A Battell of Birds most strangly fought in Ireland upon the 8th day of September, 1621, where neere unto the City of Corke, by the river Lee, were gathered together such a multytude of Stares, or Starlings, as the like for number was never seene in any age. To the tune of *Shore's Wife*, or to the tune of *Bonny Nell*." And in the same, iii. 124 (or Roxburghe, i. 84), another "to an excellent new tune, or to be sung to *Bonny Nell*," which commences:—

> "As I went forth one summer's day,
> To view the meadows fresh and gay," &c.

## THE LASS OF CUMBERLAND.

MS. (1670) in the Music School Collection, Oxford; 180 *Loyal Songs*, 1685 and 1694; *Apollo's Banquet*; *Pills to purge Melancholy*, all editions.

This ballad is in the Pepys Collection, iv. 25; also in the Douce Collection, p. 43, where it is entitled "Cumberland Nelly; or, The North Country Lovers," &c.

> "There was a lass of Cumberland,
> A bonny lass of high degree:
> There was a lass, her name was Nell,
> The blithest lass that e'er you see."

In the same collection, p. 44, is "Cumberland Laddy; or, Willy and Nelly of the North"; to the same tune. The first printed by J. Conyers, at the Black Raven in Duck Lane, the second by Coles, Vere, Wright, and Clarke.

In 180 *Loyal Songs*, p. 219, is "The Creditors' Complaint against the Bankers; or, The Iron Chest the Best Security:—

> "'Since Bankers are grown so brittle of late,
> That money and bankers together are flown,
> I'll chest up my money; and then, 'spite of fate,
> Let 'em all break their necks—my money's my own.'

"To the tune of *There was a Lass of Cumberland.*" It consists of ten stanzas, and commences:—

> "Bankers are now such brittle ware,
> They break just like a Venice glass;
> If you trust them, then have a care,
> Lest your coins to foreign lands do pass.
>
> *An iron chest is still the best,*
> *'Twill keep your coin more safe than they,*
> *For, when they've feather'd well their nest,*
> *Then the rooks will fly away.*"

In the same collection are two on James II., then Duke of York. The first, p. 176, "The Honour of great York and Albany. To *a new tune.*" The second, p. 177, "Loyalty respected, and Faction confounded. To *an excellent new tune.*" The music of *There was a Lass of Cumberland* is printed as the tune in question. The last commences with the line:—

> "Let the canons roar from sea to shore."

In the Roxburghe Collection, ii. 368, is "The Northern Lad; or, The Fair Maid's Choice, who refused all for a Plowman, counting herself therein most happy, &c. To the tune of *There was a Lass in Cumberland.*" The printer's name is cut off this copy, which is a version of the ballad differing from that in the *Pills* and the Douce Collection. It commences:—

> "I am a lass o' th' North Countrey,
> And I was born and bred a-whome."

There is another to the tune in the Pepys Collection, iii. 167, called 'The Yeoman's Delight," &c., beginning:—

> "For Katy, Katy, Katy O,
> The love I bear to Katy O," &c.

## CAVALILLY MAN.

*The Dancing Master,* 1670, &c.; 180 *Loyal Songs,* 1685 and 1694; *Pills to purge Melancholy,* ii. 18, and iii. 65, 1707; *The Village Opera,* and others.

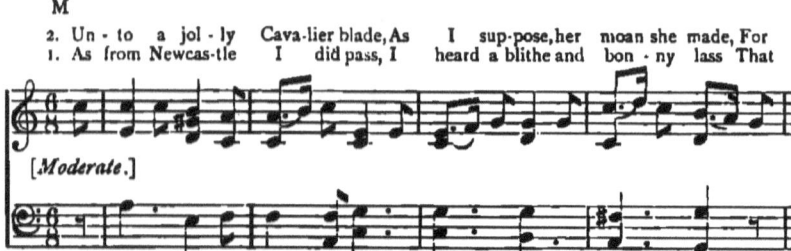

The words are taken from the original ballad in Mr. Halliwell's Collection. It is entitled "The North-country Maid's Resolution, and Love to her Sweetheart. To *a pleasant new Northern tune.*" "Printed for F. Grove on Snow Hill." It consists of eleven stanzas of eight lines, besides the following burthen of four, to each verse:—

> "O my dainty Cavalilly man,
> My finnikin Cavalilly man,
> For God's cause and the Protestants',
> I prithee le' me gang with thee, man."

In the Pepys Collection, iii., p. 281, is "The well-shaped West Country Lass, set forth in her proper shapes and qualities. To the tune of *Cavalilly Man;*" beginning:—

> "Hi-ho, my heart it is light!"

And v., p. 218, "Roger, the West Country Lad, set forth in his proper shapes, or the West Country Lasses Sweet-Heart described, in answer to the well-shaped Country Lass. To the tune of *Cavalilly Man*" (2 *lines of music*); beginning:—

"Hie, hoe, pray, what shall I doe?"
*Burden:* "And this is my love, do you like him hoe?"

Printed for James Gilbertson and G. Conyers.

In Harl. MSS., No. 6,913, is a satirical song by Lord Rochester, to this tune; commencing:—

"Have you heard of a Lord of noble descent,
Hark! how the bells of Paradise ring;
As a mask of his valour, to Tangier he went," &c.

In 120 *Loyal Songs*, 1614, are the following:—

P. 196, "A new Litany to be sung in all Conventicles, for instruction of the Whigs. Tune, *Cavalilly Man*"; commencing:—

"From councils of six, when treason prevails."

P. 213, "A Song of The Light of the nation turn'd into darkness. Tune called *Cavalilly Man*"; commencing:—

"Come, all you caballers and parliament votes."

In the editions of 1685 and 1694 are several other songs, and the tune is, in one instance, entitled *Which nobody can deny*. The song is on Titus Oates. "Oates well thrashed; being a dialogue between a country farmer and his man, Jack." The first stanza, and one other end with the line, "Which nobody can deny, sir"; from which, I assume, the name is (improperly) given to the tune.

## THE FIT'S UPON ME NOW.

*The Dancing Master*, 7th edition; later called also "The Bishop of Chester's Jig."

This song is quoted by Valentine in Beaumont and Fletcher's *Wit without Money*, act v., sc. 4, where a verse is printed.

## THE DELIGHTS OF THE BOTTLE.

Matthew Lock's English Opera, *Psyche*, 1675.

Love and wine are the bonds that fasten us all,
The world, but for these, to confusion would fall:
Were it not for the pleasures of love and good wine,
Mankind for each trifle their lives would resign;
They'd not value dull life, nor could live without thinking,
Nor would kings rule the world, but for love and good drinking.

[The bass of the above setting, and the four parts of the chorus, are taken from the score of the opera, sold for the author "by John Carr at his shop at the Middle Temple Gate in Fleet Street, 1675."—ED.]

In its original form, this was a song, sung by Bacchus, in the last act of Shadwell's opera, *Psyche*, the music of which is by Matthew Lock. Shadwell wrote but two stanzas, and as that would have been too short for a ballad, some balladmonger lengthened it into twelve. A copy will be found in the Roxburghe Collection (ii. 106), containing five stanzas in the first part, and seven in the second. The tune is there described as "a most admirable new tune, everywhere much in request."

Playford printed the song in his *Choice Ayres* (omitting the chorus); and it was arranged as a duet for his *Pleasant Musical Companion* (book ii., 2nd edit., 1687). The words are also contained in the *Antidote to Melancholy*, 1682.

In the Roxburghe Collection, iii. 188, is "The Prodigal Son Converted; or, The young man returned from his ramble," &c. : "To a pleasant new playhouse tune, called *The Delights of the Bottle*." "London, printed for R. Burton, at the Horse-shoe in West Smithfield." It commences :—

"The delights and pleasures
Of a man without care."

In the same Collection, iii. 244, is a ballad on the Customs duty imposed upon French wines, dated 1681, and entitled "The Wine Cooper's Delight ": to the tune of *The Delights of the Bottle*. "Printed for the Protestant Ballad Singers." This is also in the *Collection of* 180 *Loyal Songs*, 1685 and 1694, p. 183. It consists of sixteen stanzas, commencing, "The delights of the bottle are turn'd out of doors."

There are several other ballads extant, which were to be sung to the tune.

## IN JANUARY LAST.

Playford's *Choice Ayres*, ii. 46, 1679; *Wit and Drollery*, 1682; *Pills to purge Melancholy*, vol. 1 of all editions; *Apollo's Banquet*, 1690, &c.

This is a song in D'Urfey's play, *The Fond Husband, or The Plotting Sisters*, which was acted in 1676.

The words are in the Roxburghe Collection, ii. 414, entitled "The Scotch Wedding; or, A short and pretty way of wooing: To a new Northern tune, much us'd at the theatres." Printed for P. Brooksby. In the same collection, iii. 116, is "The New-married Scotch Couple; or, The Second Part of the Scotch Wedding," &c.: "To a new Northern tune, or *In January last.*" Printed by Thackeray, Passinger, and Whitwood. A copy is also in the Douce Collection, ii. 193.

Many other ballads were sung to it, of which one or two have already been quoted. I will only add to the list, "Northern Nanny; or, The Loving Lasse's Lamentation," &c., a copy of which is in the Douce Collection, 164. It commences :—

"On Easter Monday last,    I heard a pensive maiden mourn,
When lads and lasses play,    Tears trickling down amain;
As o'er the green I past    'Alas!' quoth she, 'why was I born
Near noon-time of the day,    To live in mickle pain?'"

This identifies *In January last* as *one* of the tunes called *Northern Nanny*.

## THE CLEAR CAVALIER.

Charles Morgan's MS., dated 1682; John Banister's *Division Violin*, MS.; *Apollo's Banquet for the Treble Violin;* The ballad-opera of *Love in a Riddle*, 1729, &c. Introduced as "The Card Dance," in Mrs. Behn's farce, *The Emperor of the Moon* 1687.

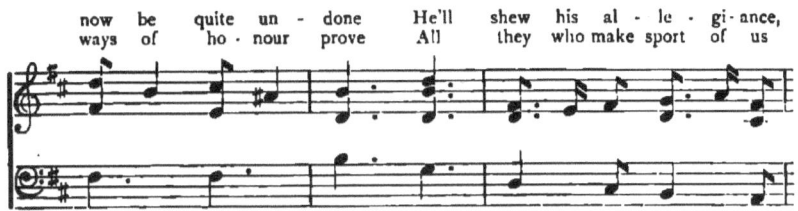

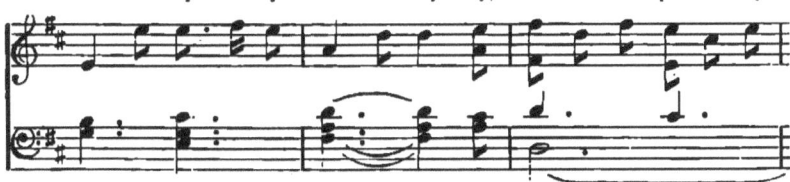

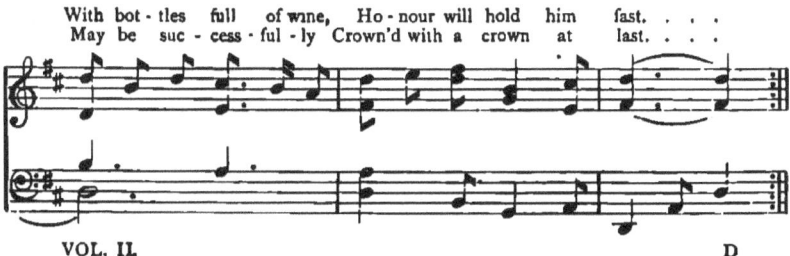

Freely let's be then honest men, and kick at Fate,
For we shall live to see our loyalty be valued at high rate;
He that bears a sword, or says a word against the throne—
That doth profanely prate against the state, no loyalty can own.
What though plumbers, painters, players, now be prosperous men,
Let us but mind our own affairs, and they'll come round again.
Treach'ry may in face look bright, and lech'ry clothe in fur;
A traitor may be made a knight, 'tis *fortune de la guerre*.
But what is that to us, boys, that are right honest men?
We'll conquer and come again, beat up the drum again,—
Hey for Cavaliers, ho for Cavaliers, drink for Cavaliers, fight for Cavaliers,
Dub-a-dub, dub-a-dub, have at old Beelzebub, Oliver quakes for fear.
Fifth Monarchy must down, boys, and every sect in town;
We'll rally and to't again, give 'em the rout again;
Fly, like light about, face to the right about, charge 'em home again, seize our own again:
Tantara, rara, and this is the life of an honest, bold Cavalier.

This is the "effusion of loyal enthusiasm" which Sir Walter Scott puts into the mouth of Sir Geoffrey Peveril, in his novel, *Peveril of the Peak*. The same lines are quoted by Shadwell in his *Epsom Wells*, where Fribble says to the fiddlers, "Can't you sing—

> ' Hey for Cavaliers, ho for Cavaliers,
> Dub-a-dub-dub, have at old Beelzebub,
> Oliver quakes for fear.' "—*Act v., sc.* 1.

The song is attributed to Samuel Butler, author of *Hudibras*, and is printed in his *Posthumous Works;* also in *Westminster Drollery*, part ii., p. 48, 1672; in *Loyal Songs written against the Rump Parliament*, i. 249; in *Pills to purge Melancholy*, &c.

## THE FAIR ONE LET ME IN.

D'Urfey's *New Collection*, &c., 1683; *Choice Ayres*, &c., 1683; *Pills to purge Melancholy*, all editions; many Ballad Operas.

The words of the original song, "The night her blackest sables wore," or "The fair one let me in," were published in "A New Collection of Songs and Poems, by Thomas D'Urfey, gent. Printed for Joseph Hindmarsh, at the Black Bull, in Cornhill," 1683 (8vo); and there entitled, "The Generous Lover, a new song, set by Mr. Tho. Farmer."

A black-letter copy of this song in ballad form, in the Roxburghe Collection, ii. 240, is entitled, "Kind Lady, or the Loves of Stella and Adonis: A new court song, much in request. To a *new tune*, or *Hey, boys, up go we, The Charming Nymph*, or *Jenny, gin*." It commences:—

"The night her blackest sables wore," &c.

The "new tune" soon became popular, and many other ballads were sung to it. In the same volume of the Roxburghe Collection are "The Good Fellow's Frolic, or Kent Street Club: to the tune of *The fair one let me in*," p. 198; "The Love-sick Maid of Wapping," p. 295; and a third ballad at p. 270.

In the Douce Collection, p. 55, is "The despairing Maiden reviv'd by the return of her dearest love," &c.: "to the tune of *The fair one let me in,* or *Busy Fame,* or *Jenny, gin*"; commencing:—

> "As I walkt forth to take the air,
> One morning in the spring,
> And for to view the lilies fair,
> To hear the small birds sing," &c.

In the Halliwell Collection, No. 180 (p. 66 of catalogue), and in Roxburghe, vol. ii., p. 270, will be found, "The Life of Love:—

> ' Let he or she, from chains if free,
> Prize high their liberty,
> Love's a disease that seems to please,
> Yet breeds captivity.'

To the tune of *The fair one let me in,* or *Busy Fame.* Printed for P. Brooksby, at the Golden Ball, in Pye Corner."

The Roxburghe Collection also contains the following:—Vol. ii., p. 104, "The Deptford Frolick." Tune, *The fair one let me in* (P. Brooksby). Vol. ii., p. 156, "Fair Lucina conquer'd by prevailing Cupid," &c. Tune of *Jenny, gin,* or *The fair one let me in;* beginning:—

> "Lucina sitting in her bow'r,
> Was wounded with a dart."

Vol. ii., p. 320, "Loyal Constancy; or, The Seamen's Love-letter," &c. Tune of *Cloris full of harmless thought, Jenny, gin,* or *The fair one let me in;* beginning "Till from Leghorn I do return," and an answer to the same tune.

Although there can be no doubt of the authorship of the words and music of this song, it has been claimed as Scotch.


## YOUNG JEMMY.

*The Genteel Companion for the Recorder,* 1683; 180 *Loyal Songs,* 1683 and 1694; *The Village Opera,* 1729; *Love and Revenge, or The Vintner Outwitted,* N.D.; *The Bay's Opera,* 1730, &c.

M.

## THE LATER POPULAR MUSIC.

There are two copies of this ballad; one in the King's Library, Brit. Mus. entitled "Young Jemmy: An excellent new Ballad. To *an excellent new tune*," dated 1681; and the second in the Roxburghe Collection, ii. 140, called "England's Darling; or, Great Britain's Joy and Hope in that noble Prince, James, Duke of Monmouth:

> 'Brave Monmouth, England's glory,
> Hated of none but Papist and Tory,
> May'st thou in thy noble father's love remain,
> Who happily over this land doth reign.'

Tune of *Young Jemmy*, or *Philander*." Printed by J. Wright, J. Clarke, W. Thackeray, and T. Passinger. It commences:—

" Young Jemmy is a lad  
   That's royally descended,  
With every virtue clad,  
   By every tongue commended ;

A true and faithful English heart,  
   Great Britain's joy and hope,  
And bravely will maintain their part,  
   In spite of Turk and Pope," &c.[1]

---

This is printed in Mrs. Aphra Behn's *Poems upon several Occasions*, 1684, as a "Song to a new Scotch tune."

"To a *new Play-house tune*, or *In January last*, or *The Gowlin.*" Printed by P. Brooksby, at the Golden Ball, in West Smithfield (Rox. ii. 556). Commencing :—

> "Young Jemmy was a lad
>     Of royal birth and breeding,
> With every beauty clad,
>     And every swain exceeding :
>
> A face and shape so wondrous fine,
>     So charming every part,
> That every lass upon the green
>     For Jemmy had a heart," &c.

Both these ballads have been reprinted in Evans's Collection, iii. 206 and 211, 1810.

There are two others to the tune in 180 *Loyal Songs;* the first, "Old Jemmy, tune of *Young Jemmy.*" It is a counter-panegyric upon James II., when Duke of York, by Mat. Tauban, commencing :—

> "Old Jemmy is a lad
>     Right lawfully descended."

The second, "A new song on the arrival of Prince George [of Denmark], and his intermarriage with the Lady Anne," afterwards Queen Anne ; commencing :—

> " Prince George at last is come ;
>     Fill every man his bumper," &c.

In the Roxburghe Collection, ii. 504, is " The West-country Nymph ; or, The Loyal Maid of Bristol," &c. : to the tune of *Young Jemmy;* beginning :—

> "Come, all you maidens fair,
>     And listen to my ditty ;
> In Bristol city fair
>     There liv'd a damsel pretty."

In the early part of the last century, the Pretender was called "Young Jemmy," and the tune became a favourite with the Jacobites. " I never can pass through Cranbourn Alley, but I am astonished at the remissness or lenity of the magistrates in suffering the Pretender's interest to be carried on and promoted in so public and shameful a manner as it there is. Here a fellow stands eternally bawling out his Pye-Corner pastorals in behalf of *Dear Jemmy, Lovely Jemmy,*" &c.—(*A View of London and Westminster,* &c., " by a German gentleman," 2nd ed., 1725.)

## WHEN BUSY FAME.

Playford's *Choice Ayres*, v. 19, 1684; *Pills to purge Melancholy*, iii. 249, 1707, and v. 164, 1719.

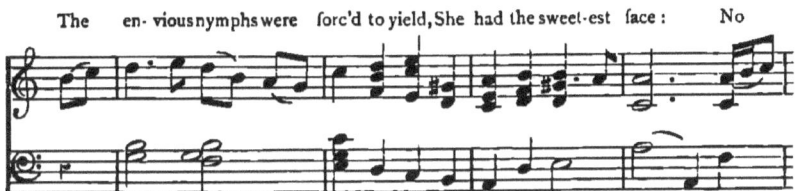

   Young Coridon, whose stubborn heart
    No beauty e'er could move,
   That smil'd at Cupid's bow and dart,
    And brav'd the God of Love,
   Would view this nymph, and pleas'd, at first,
    Such silent charms to see,
   With wonder gaz'd, then sigh'd, and curs'd
    His curiosity.

40    THE LATER POPULAR MUSIC.

This tune, which was composed by T. Farmer, was popular in the latter part of the reign of Charles II., and continued in favour for at least half a century. Several ballads that were to be sung to it have already been mentioned. The following are in the Halliwell Collection :—

No. 47, " Coridon and Parthenia, the languishing shepherd made happy, or faithful love rewarded, being a most pleasant and delectable new Play Song—

> ' Here mournful love is turn'd into delight,
> To this we a chaste amorist invite.' "

To the tune of *When busy Fame*. Printed for F. Coles, T. Vere, J. Wright, J. Clarke, W. Thackeray, and T. Passinger. Also another copy printed by P. Brooksby.

No. 180, " The Life of Love," &c. : " to the tune of *The fair one let me in*, or *Busy Fame*." Printed for P. Brooksby, &c.

No. 349, " The Trepanned Virgin ; or, Good Advice to Maidens," &c. " Tune, *When busie Fame*." Printed for Coles, Vere, Wright, &c.

The first and third of these ballads will also be found in vol. ii. of the Roxburghe Collection, at pp. 68 and 455. Others to the tune will be found in the same volume, at pp. 45, 224, and 322.

In the Pepys Collection, iv. 103, and Roxburghe, vol. ii., p. 7, is " Advice to Batchelors, &c.: to the tune of *Hey, boys, up go we, Busie Fame, Marrellus*, or *Jenny, Gin*." (J. Deacon at the Angel.) It begins :—

> " You batchelors that single are
> May lead a happy life."

## COCK LORREL.

180 *Loyal Songs*, 1685 ; *Pills to purge Melancholy; The Dancing Master*, 1650, &c.

In *The Dancing Master* it is called by another name, from a song, of which four lines are quoted in Rowley's *A Match at Midnight*, act i., sc. 1, and one in Shirley's *The Constant Maid*, act ii., sc. 2, where the usurer's niece sings it.

The song of "Cock Lorrel" is in Ben Jonson's masque, *The Gipsies Metamorphosed*. Copies are also in the Pepys Collection of Ballads; in Dr. Percy's folio MS., p. 182; and, with music, in *Pills to purge Melancholy*. It is a satire upon rogues and knaves of all classes.[1]

In *Satirical Poems*, by Lord Rochester (Harl. MSS., 6,913), there is a ballad to the tune; and in the "Collection of Loyal Songs written against the Rump Parliament" there are many, such as " The Rump roughly but righteously handled"; "The City's Feast to the Lord Protector"; "St. George for England" (commencing, "The Westminster Rump hath been little at ease"), &c., &c. Others in the King's Pamphlets, Brit. Mus.; in the *Collection of* 180 *Loyal Songs*, 1685; in *Poems on Affairs of State*, vol. i., 1703; and in the Roxburghe Collection of Ballads.

A tune called *The Painter* is sometimes mentioned, and it appears to be another name for this air, because the ballad of "The Painter's Pastime; or, A woman defined after a new fashion," &c., was to be sung to the tune of *Cock Laurel*. A black-letter copy is in the Douce Collection (printed by P. Brooksby, at the Golden Ball, &c.).

*Michaelmas-Term*, *The Rambling Clerke*, and *A Bill of Fare* are also names acquired by the tune from ballads to which it was sung.

---

[1] Wynken de Worde printed a tract called *Cocke Lorrell's Bote*, in which persons of all classes, and among them the *Mynstrelles*, are summoned to go on board his Ship of Fools. *Cock Lorel's Boa.* is mentioned in a MS. poem in the Bodleian Library, called *Doctour Double Ale*, and in John Heywood's *Epigrams upon* 300 *Proverbs*, 1566 (in the Epigram upon a Busy-body, No. 189).

In S. Rowland's *Martin Markhall, his Defence and Answer to the Bellman of London*, 1610, is a list of rogues by profession, in which *Cock Lorrel* stands second. He is thus described: "After him succeeded, by the general council, one Cock Lorrell, the most notorious knave that ever lived. By trade he was a tinker, often carrying a pan and hammer for show; but when he came to a good booty, he would cast his profession in a ditch, and play the padder." In 1565 a book was printed called *The Fraternitye of Vacabondes; whereunto also is adjoyned the twenty-five orders of knaves: confirmed for ever by Cocke Lorell.*

## A BEGGING WE WILL GO.

*Choice Ayres*, &c., 1685; *Loyal Songs*, 1685; *The Quaker's Opera*, and many others.

There was a jovial beggar,
 He had a wooden leg,
Lame from his cradle,
 And forced for to beg.
And a begging we will go, we'll go, we'll go,
And a begging we will go!

 A bag for his oatmeal,
  Another for his salt;
 And a pair of crutches
  To show that he can halt.
   And a begging, &c.

 A bag for his wheat,
  Another for his rye;
 A little bottle by his side
  To drink when he's a dry.
   And a begging, &c.

 Seven years I begg'd
  For my old master *Wild*,
 He taught me to beg
  When I was but a child.
   And a begging, &c.

 I begg'd for my master,
  And got him store of pelf;
 But now, Jove be praised,
  I'm begging for myself.
   And a begging, &c.

 In a hollow tree
  I live, and pay no rent;
 Providence provides for me,
  And I am well content.
   And a begging, &c.

 Of all the occupations
  A beggar's life's the best;
 For whene'er he's weary,
  He'll lay him down and rest.
   And a begging, &c.

 I fear no plots against me,
  I live in open cell;
 Then who would be a king
  When beggars live so well?
And a begging we will go, we'll go, we'll go,
And a begging we will go!

In the Bagford Collection a copy of this song, in black-letter, is entitled "The Beggars' Chorus in *The Jovial Crew: to an excellent new tune*." Brome's comedy, *The Jovial Crew; or, The Merry Beggars*, was acted at the Cockpit in Drury Lane, in 1641, and I suppose the song to have been introduced, as it is not contained in the printed copy of the play. The stanza, "Of all the occupations," &c., is quoted by Cotgrave in his *French and English Dictionary*, 1611 (under the word "*Vie*").

One of the Cavaliers' ditties, "Col. John Okie's Lamentations; or, A Rumper cashiered," is to the tune of *A begging we will go*. This was published on the 28th March, 1660, and a copy may be seen among the King's Pamphlets, Brit. Mus.

"A begging we will go" is printed, with the music, in book v. of *Choice Ayres and Songs to sing to the Theorbo or Bass Viol*, fol. 1684; in 180 *Loyal Songs*, 3rd edit., 1685; in *Pills to purge Melancholy*, &c. It is sometimes entitled "The Jovial Beggars."

The song is the prototype of many others, such as "A bowling we will go," "A fishing we will go," "A hawking we will go," and "A hunting we will go."

### I'LL TELL THEE, DICK, WHERE I HAVE BEEN.

*Loyal Songs*, 1685; *Pills to purge Melancholy*, vol. i., 1699 and 1707.

M.
I'll tell thee, Dick, where I have been, Where I the rar - est things have

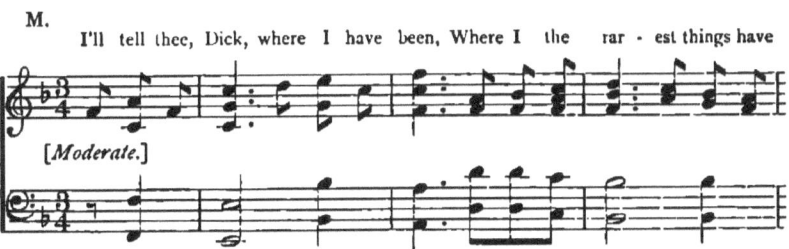

[*Moderate.*]

seen, Oh! things be-yond com-pare. Such sights a - gain can-not be

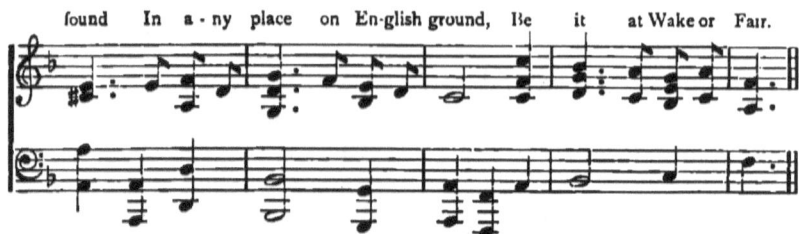

At Charing Cross, hard by the way
Where we, thou know'st, do sell our hay,
There is a house with stairs;
And there did I see coming down
Such folk as are not in our town,
Forty, at least, in pairs, &c.

This celebrated ballad, by Sir John Suckling, was occasioned by the marriage of Roger Boyle, the first Earl of Orrery (then Lord Broghill), with Lady Margaret Howard, daughter of the Earl of Suffolk. The words are in the first edition of Sir John Suckling's works, 1646; in *Wit's Recreation*, 1654; in *Merry Drollery Complete*, 1661; *Antidote to Melancholy*, 1661; in *The Convivial Songster*, 1782; in Ritson's *Ancient Songs*, p. 223; and Ellis' *Specimens of Early English Poets*, iii. 248.

The following were written to the tune :—

1. "The Cavalier's Complaint." A copy in the Bagford Collection (643, m. 11, p. 23), dated 1660; and one in the King's Pamphlets, No. 19, fol., 1661; others in *Antidote to Melancholy; Merry Drollery Complete*, 1670; *The New Academy of Compliments*, 1694 and 1713; and Dryden's *Miscellany Poems*, vi. 352, &c.

"Come, Jack, let's drink a pot of ale,
And I will tell thee such a tale,
Shall make thine ears to ring."

2. "An Echo to the Cavalier's Complaint." Copies in *The Antidote to Melancholy*, 1661; *Merry Drollery Complete*, 1670; *New Academy of Compliments*, &c.

"I marvel, Dick, that having been
So long abroad, and having seen
The world, as thou hast done,
Thou shouldst acquaint me with a tale," &c.

3. "Upon Sir John Suckling's 100 Horse." Contained in *Le Prince d'Amour; or, The Prince of Love*, 1660, p. 148.

4 and 5. "A Ballad on a Friend's Wedding," and "Three Merry Boys of Kent," in *Folly in Print; or, A Book of Rhymes*, 1667.

6. "A new Ballad, called The Chequers Inn." in *Poems on State Affairs*, iii. 57, 1704. It begins:—

> "I tell thee, Dick, where I have been,
> Where I the Parliament have seen," &c.

7. "A Christmas Song," when the Rump Parliament was first dissolved, *Loyal Songs*, ii. 99, 1731.

Besides these, there is one in Carey's *Trivial Poems*, 1651; three in 180 *Loyal Songs*, 1685, &c.

## ROGER OF COVERLY.

Playford's *Division Violin*, 1685; *The Dancing Master*, 1696, &c.; many Ballad Operas, &c.

This tune, in its original form, is at least as early as the reign of Charles I. This appears from a tract in the King's Pamphlets (Brit. Mus. e. 435, No. 44, p. 15) printed in 1648, giving an account of a quarrel between a Sir Hugh Calverley and Mr. John Griffiths, in the county of Cheshire, where it is thus referred to:—"I made the fiddler play a tune called *Roger of Caulveley* from one end of the town to the other. This I did to shew that I did not fear to be disarmed by them."[1]

There is a song with the burden, "O brave Roger a Cauverly," in *Pills to purge Melancholy*, vi. 31 ; and which I suppose should be to the tune, although four bars of *Old Sir Simon the King* are printed above it. Both are in 9/4 time. It commences very abruptly, as if it were a fragment, instead of an entire song.

" She met with a countryman
  In the middle of all the Green ;
And Peggy was his delight,
  And good sport was to be seen.
But ever she cried, Brave Roger,
  I'll drink a whole glass to thee ;

But as for John of the Green,
  I care not a pin for he.
*Bulls and bears, and lions and dragons,*
  *And O brave Roger a Cauverly;*
*Piggins and wiggins, pints and flagons,*
  *O brave Roger a Cauverly.*"

It is mentioned as one which "the hob-nailed fellows" call for, in *The History of Robert Powel, the Puppet-showman*, 8vo, 1715. " Upon the preludes being ended, each party fell to bawling and calling for particular tunes. The hob-nail'd fellows, whose breeches and lungs seem'd to be of the same leather, cried out for *Cheshire Rounds, Roger of Coverly, Joan's Placket*, and *Northern Nancy*."

---

[1] According to Ralph Thoresby's MS. account of the family of Calverley, of Calverley, in Yorkshire, the dance of *Roger de Coverley* was named after a knight who lived in the reign of Richard I. Thoresby was born in 1658. The following extract from his manuscript was communicated to *Notes and Queries*, i. 369, by Sir Walter Calverley Trevelyan, Bart. :—" Roger, so named from the Archbishop [of York], was a person of renowned hospitality, since, at this day, *the obsolete known tune of Roger a Calverley* is referred to him, who, according to the custom of those times, kept his Minstrels, from that, their office, named Harpers, which became a family, and possessed lands till late years in and about Calverley, called to this day *Harpersroids* and *Harper's Spring*."

## WHEN THE STORMY WINDS DO BLOW.

The Ballad Broadsides; *Loyal Songs*, 1686, &c.

The sailor must have courage,
   No danger he must shun ;
In every kind of weather
   His course he still must run ;
Now mounted on the top-mast,
   How dreadful 'tis below :
Then we ride, as the tide,
   When the stormy winds do blow.

If enemies oppose us.
   And England is at war
With any foreign nation,
   We fear not wound nor scar.
To humble them, come on, lads,
   Their flags we'll soon lay low ;
Clear the way for the fray,
   Tho' the stormy winds do blow

Sometimes in Neptune's bosom
   Our ship is toss'd by waves,
And every man expecting
   The sea to be our graves ;
Then up aloft she's mounted,
   And down again so low,
In the waves, on the seas,
   When the stormy winds do blow.

But when the danger's over,
   And safe we come on shore,
The horrors of the tempest
   We think of then no more ;
The flowing bowl invites us,
   And joyfully we go,
All the day drink away,
   Tho' the stormy winds do blow.

The ballad, now known as *You Gentlemen of England*, is an alteration of one by M[artin] P[arker], a copy of which is in the Pepys Collection, i. 420 ; printed at London for C. Wright. It is in black-letter, and entitled " Saylers for my money : a new ditty composed in the praise of Saylers and Sea Affaires ; briefly shewing the nature of so worthy a calling, and effects of their industry : to the manner of their rejoycing on shore, at their return home. Tune of *When the stormy winds do blow*" (the burden of the song). A black-letter copy of this version is in the Bagford Collection, printed by W. O[nley], *temp.* Charles II. ; and in one of the volumes of the Douce Collection, p. 168, printed by C. Brown and T. Norris, and sold at the Looking Glass on London Bridge. A third is in the Roxburghe Collection, ii. 543. " Stormy Winds " is also in the list of ballads printed by W. Thackeray, about 1660. No early copy of the tune is known.

On the accession of Charles II., we have, " The Valiant Seaman's Congratulation to his Sacred Majesty King Charles the Second," &c.: " to the tune of *Let us drink and sing, and merrily troul the bowl*, or *The stormy winds do blow*, or *Hey, ho, my honey*." (Black-letter, twelve stanzas ; F. Grove, Snow Hill.) It commences thus :—

    " Great Charles, your English seamen,
      Upon our bended knee,
    Present ourselves as freemen
      Unto your Majesty.
    Beseeching God to bless you
      Where ever that you go ;
    So we pray, night and day,
      When the stormy winds do blow."

Although the option of singing it to three tunes is given, it is evident, from the two last lines, that it was written to this.

Among the other ballads to the tune are, "The Valiant Virgin, or Philip and Mary: In a description of a young gentlewoman of Worcestershire (a rich gentleman's daughter) being in love with a farmer's son, which her father despising, because he was poor, caus'd him to be press'd for sea: and how she disguised herself in man's apparel and follow'd him," &c.: "to the tune of *When the stormy winds do blow*"; (Roxburghe, ii. 546) beginning :—

"To every faithful lover
That's constant to her dear," &c.

In *Poems by Ben Jonson, junior*, 8vo, 1672, is "The Bridegroom's Salutation: to the tune *When the stormy winds do blow*"; beginning :—

"I took thee on a suddain,
In all thy glories drest," &c.

In 180 *Loyal Songs*, 1686 and 1694, a bad version of the tune is printed to "You Calvinists of England."

In Halliwell's Catalogue, p. 36 (No. 103), is "England's Valour and Holland's Terrour, being an encouragement for seamen and souldiers to serve His Majesty in his wars against the Dutch," &c.: "to the tune of *The Stormy Winds do blow*."

In the Pepys Collection, vol. i., 418 (No. 215), is "The praise of sailors here set forth, with their hard fortunes which doe befall them on the seas, when land-men sleep safe in their beds: to a *pleasant new tune*." Printed for J. Wright. It begins :—

"As I lay musing in my bed,
Full warm and well at ease,
I thought upon the lodging hard
Poor sailors have at seas."

## THE KING'S JIG, OR AT WINCHESTER WAS A WEDDING.

*The Dancing Master*, 1686, &c.; *Pills to purge Melancholy;* 180 *Loyal Songs;* and many of the Ballad Operas.

The dancing of jigs is now in a great measure confined to Ireland; but they were formerly equally common in England and Scotland. The word "jig" is said to be derived from the Anglo-Saxon, and in Old English literature its application extended, beyond the tune itself, to any jigging rhymes that might be sung to such tunes. The songs sung by clowns after plays (which, like those of Tarleton, were often extempore), and any other merry ditties, were called jigs. "Nay, sit down by my side, and I will *sing* thee one of my countrey jigges to make thee merry," says Deloney, in his *Thomas of Reading;* and Will. Kempe, the comedian and Morris dancer, wrote "A new jigg of the *Kitchenstuff-Woman*," and "A new jigg betwixt a soldier, a miser, and Sym the clowne."

Heywood includes jigs among the dances of the country people, in the following passage from *A Woman killed with Kindness* :—

> " Now, gallants, while the town musicians
> Finger their frets within, and the mad lads
> And country lasses, every mother's child,
> With nosegays and bride-laces in their hats,
> Dance all their country measures, rounds, and jigs," &c.

Jigs, however, were danced by persons of all ranks during the latter half of the seventeenth century ; and this having been published as *The King's Jig*, during the life of Charles II., we may suppose it to be one of the tunes to which his Majesty danced. The jigs of the Inner Temple, the Middle Temple, Lincoln's Inn, Gray's Inn, and many others, are to be found in the editions of *Apollo's Banquet for the Treble Violin*, printed in this and the following reign.

D'Urfey wrote a descriptive song called "The Winchester Wedding: set to *The King's Jigg*, a Country Dance"; and it was published, with the tune, among " Several new Songs by Tho. D'Urfey, Gent., set to as many new tunes by the best masters in music," fol., 1684. It became very popular, was printed as a penny ballad, and the tune became better known as *The Winchester Wedding* than as *The King's Jig.*

Among the ballads that were sung to the tune, I have already quoted one, printed in July, 1685, " On the Virgins of Taunton Dean, who ript open their silk petticoats to make colours for the late D[uke] of M[onmouth]'s army." It commences :—

> ' In Lime began a rebellion,
>    For there the rebels came in ;
> Rebels, almost a million,
>    Came there to make M[onmouth] King."

And there are many others, such as " A Fairing for Young Men and Maids" (Roxburghe Collection, ii. 162), &c.

## THE TWENTY-NINTH OF MAY.

*The Dancing Master*, 1686, and all subsequent editions.

In several editions of *The Dancing Master* this tune is printed twice, the second copy being under another name. For instance, in the "Additional Sheet" to the edition of 1686 it appears as *May Hill, or The Jovial Crew;* in "The Second Part" of that of 1698 as *The Jovial Beggars;* in the third volume of *The Dancing Master*, N.D. (a later publication), as the *Restoration of King Charles.*

It also bears the name of *The Jovial Crew* in *Apollo's Banquet for the Treble Violin.*

## OH, HOW THEY FRISK IT, OR LEATHER APRON, OR UNDER THE GREENWOOD TREE.

*The Dancing Master*, 1686, &c.; *Pills to purge Melancholy;* and many Ballad Operas.

M.

1. In Summer time, when flow'rs do spring, And birds sit on each tree, . . Let

[*Moderate.*]

Lords and Knights say what they will, There's none so merry as we. . . There's

Will and Moll, with Har - ry and Doll, And Tom and bonny Bet - tee, Oh! . .

how they do jerk it, Ca - per and firk it, Un-der the greenwood tree. In

Our music is a little pipe,
That can so sweetly play;
We hire Old *Hal* from Whitsuntide
Till latter Lammas-day;
On Sabbath days and holy-days
After ev'ning prayer comes he; [1]
And then do we skip it, caper and trip it,
Under the green-wood tree.
In summer time, &c.

Come, play us *Adam and Eve*, says Dick;
What's that? says little Pipe;
*The Beginning of the World*, quoth Dick;
For we are dancing-ripe;
Is't that you call? then *have at all*—
He play'd with merry glee;
O then did we skip it, caper and trip it,
Under the green-wood tree.
In summer time, &c.

There are two versions of this tune in *The Dancing Master* of 1686 —the first in common, and the second in ⁶⁄₄ time: the first entitled *Under the Greenwood Tree*, the second (in the additional sheet), *Oh! how they frisk it*, or *Leather Apron*.

I have only observed two other copies in common time. One is in *The Dancing Master* of 1690 (in all later editions, and in *Pills to purge Melancholy*, it is in ⁶⁄₄ time), and the other is Ashmole's version.

Ashmole's copy of the words differs somewhat from the black-letter ballads; and, if written at the time when he is stated to have been intent upon music—soon after his father's death in 1634—it may be from forty to fifty years older than any printed copy that I have observed, the earliest of which was published by Brooksby.[2] The words in his copy begin thus:—

---

[1] Bishop Earle, in his *Microcosmographie*, describing a "Plain countryfellow, or downright clown," says, "Sunday he esteems a day to make merry in, and thinks a bag-pipe as essential to it as evening prayer. He walks very solemnly after service, with his hands coupled behind him, and censures" (*i.e.* criticizes) "the dancing of his parish."

Burton, in his *Anatomy of Melancholy*, says: "Young lasses are never better pleased, than when, as upon a holiday, after evensong, they may meet their sweet-hearts, and dance about a May-pole, or in a Town-green, under a shady elm."

[2] The earliest date that I have noted to any ballad printed by Brooksby is April 12, 1677.

> "In summer time, when leaves grow green,
>   And birds sit on the tree,
>  Let all the lords say what they can,
>   There's none so merry as we.
>  There's Jeffry and Tom, there's Ursula and John,
>   With Roger and bonny Bettee;
>  Oh! how they do firk it, caper and jerk it,
>   *Under the Greenwood Tree.*"

The ballads of "King Edward the Fourth and the Tanner of Tamworth," and "Robin Hood and the Curtal Friar," commence precisely as in Ashmole's copy, and, the metre of all being the same, it appears very probable that they were sung to one tune, and, therefore, that this air in its original form may belong to the reign of Elizabeth. Another ancient ballad, "Robin Hood and the Monk," begins in a similar manner, and the eighth line corresponds with the burden of this ballad.

There are two black-letter copies of the ballad in the Douce Collection, where it is entitled "The West Country Delight, or Hey for Zommersetshire."

An answer to it will also be found in the Douce Collection to be sung to the same tune. It is "Hey for our town, but a fig for a Zommersetshire"; and commences:—

> " In winter time, when flow'rs do fade,
>   And birds forsake the tree,
>  Let lords and ladies play at cards,
>   There's none so merry as we," &c.

The burden is "Under the holly-bush tree."

The tune is sometimes entitled *Caper and firk it*, as in "The Fair Maid of Islington; or, The London Vintner over-reach'd: to the tune of *Sellinger's Round*, or *Caper and firk it.*"—(Bagford, 643, m. 10, p. 113.) Con mencing:—

> " There was a fair Maid of Islington,
>   As I heard many tell,
>  And she would to fair London go,
>   Fine apples and pears to sell," &c.

It is included among the tunes of Christmas Carols in "A Cabinet of Choice Jewels; or, The Christian's Joy and Gladness: set forth in sundry pleasant new Christmas Carols," 1688.

"A delightful song in honour of Whitsontide: to the tune of *Caper and jerk it*," is contained in *Canterbury Tales*, &c., printed in Bow Churchyard. It commences:—

> " Now Whitson holidays they are come
>   Each lass shall find her mate."

## MAD ROBIN.

*The Dancing Master* of 1686 (additional sheet), and in all later editions ; *Polly*, 1728 ; *The Lovers' Opera*, 1729 ; *The Stage Mutineers*, 1733 ; and many other Ballad Operas.

There is a reference to this tune in *The History of Robert Powel, the Puppet-Showman*, 8vo, 1715 :—" 'Tis but a day or two ago since our mistress turn'd away her old servant, because he would not play *Mad Robin*, which the organist has promised to do." The song (if any existed) is not known.

## JOAN'S PLACKET IS TORN.

*The Dancing Master*, 1686, &c; *The Bays' Opera, Achilles,* and *Love in a Riddle,* 1729.

The earliest notice I have found of this air is in Pepys' Diary; where, under date of 22nd June, 1667, he speaks of a trumpeter, on board the "Royal Charles," sounding the tune of *Joan's Placket is Torn*.

It is contained in *The Dancing Master* of 1686 (additional sheet), and in all subsequent editions; also in the ballad operas of *Achilles, The Bays' Opera,* and *Love in a Riddle.*

Colley Cibber's song, "When I followed a lass that was froward and shy," which was written to the tune, for *Love in a Riddle*, in 1729, was transferred by Bickerstaff to *Love in a Village* about thirty years later, without acknowledgment of the source from which he derived it.

In the collection of *Loyal Songs*, 1685 and 1694, is one entitled, " The Plot cram'd into Jone's Placket : to the tune of *Jone's Placket is*

*Torn.*" It is also one of the tunes called for by "the hob-nailed fellows" in *The History of Robert Powel, the Puppet Showman*, 8vo, 1715.

This tune may perhaps date originally from the reign of Elizabeth; for the tune given in the Rev. G. R. Gleig's *Family History of England*, and mentioned in Miss Strickland's *Mary Stuart*, as the one played by the trumpets at the execution of the Queen of Scots, is nothing but a version of *Joan's Placket*. In Miss Strickland's work the tune is also said to be the one "sung, with appropriate words, to brutalize the rabble at the burning of a witch." Neither author, however, quotes any better authority than "an old M.S.," or "tradition."

## LILLIBURLERO.

*The Delightful Companion, or Choice New Lessons for the Recorder or Flute* (by Robert Carr), 1686; *Musick's Handmaid*, 1689; *Pills to purge Melancholy*; and many Ballad Operas.

Ho! by my shoul it is de Talbot,
And he will cut all de English throat;
Tho', by my shoul, de English do praat,
De law's on dare side, and Creish knows what.

But, if dispence do come from de Pope,
We'll hang Magna Charta and demselves in a rope.

And de good Talbot is made a lord,
And he with brave lads is coming aboard,
Who all in France have tauken a sware,
Dat dey will have no Protestant heir.

O, but why does he stay behind?
Ho! by my shoul, 'tis a Protestant wind.

Now Tyrconnel is come ashore,
And we shall have commissions gillore;
And he dat will not go to mass
Shall turn out, and look like an ass.

Now, now de hereticks all go down,
By Creish and St. Patrick, de nation's our own.

Percy says of these verses, "Slight and insignificant as they may now seem, they had once a more powerful effect than either the Philippics of Demosthenes or Cicero; and contributed not a little towards the great revolution in 1688. Let us hear a contemporary writer:—

"A foolish ballad was made at that time, treating the Papists, and chiefly the Irish, in a very ridiculous manner, which had a burden, said to be Irish words, 'Lero, lero, lilliburlero,' that made an impression on the [King's] army, that cannot be imagined by those that saw it not. The whole army, and at last the people, both in city and country, were singing it perpetually. And, perhaps, never had so slight a thing so great an effect."—*Burnet's History of his own Times*.

"It was written, or at least re-published, on the Earl of Tyrconnel's going a second time to Ireland, in 1688. . . . . *Lilliburlero* and *Bullen-a-lah* are said to have been the words of distinction used among the Irish Papists in their massacre of Protestants, in 1641."

The first *collection* in which the words of *Lilliburlero* appeared was *The Muses' Farewell to Popery and Slavery*, 1689. It was afterwards published in *Poems on Affairs of State*, and some others. Percy prints but the first part.

The words have been variously ascribed to Lord Wharton and Lord Dorset, but probably neither was the author. The tune is a harpsichord lesson by Purcell, printed with his name in the second edition of *Musick's Handmaid*[1] (and would probably be found in the first also, could a copy of that edition be discovered), two years before Tyrconnel's appointment as Lord Deputy, and therefore before the ballad can have been written.

There are, of course, numerous references to the song in the literature

---

[1] In *Musick's Handmaid* it is called "A new Irish tune," and by "Mr. Purcell." Purcell also made use of it as the ground to the fifth air in his opera of *The Gordian Knot unty'd*.

of the eighteenth century, and the ballads sung to the tune were many. Among others may be mentioned:—

"Dublin's Deliverance; or, The Surrender of Drogheda": commencing, "Protestant Boys, good tidings I bring." This, singularly enough, is omitted in Mr. Crofton Croker's *Historical Songs of Ireland*. A copy is in the Pepys Collection, ii. 303.

"Undaunted London-derry; or, The Victorious Protestants' constant success against the proud French and Irish Forces": commencing, "Protestant Boys, both valiant and stout." Bagford Collection, 634, m. 10, p. 116; and in the same volume, "The Courageous Soldiers of the West," and "The Reading Skirmish."

The Roxburghe Collection contains "The Protestant Courage," "Courageous Betty of Chick Lane," &c., &c.

## THE KING OF POLAND, OR COURTIERS, COURTIERS.

With the first title in *The Dancing Master*, 1686; with the second on Broadsides, about 1695.

M.

Courtiers, Courtiers think not in scorn, If poor silly swains in love should be,

[*Moderate.*]

Love lies hid in rags all torn, As well as in silks and bra-ve-ry,

And the beg-gar doth love his lass as dear As he that hath thou-sands,

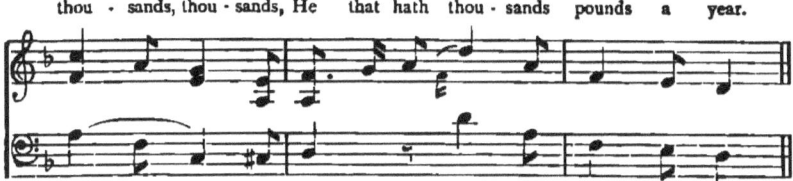

State and pomp no happiness brings,
  A lower place more joys doth prove ;
For Lords and Ladies, Princes and Kings,
  With all on a level are in love.
And pretty brown Mary, making hay,
  Hath charms as killing, killing, killing,
Always as killing charms as they.

Content's the thing that mortals doth bless
  And better far than a golden mine ;
In Mary I the world possess,
  And at no other's lot repine.
Sweet Mary to me in careless hair
  Has treasures far more taking, taking,
Than they that tow'rs and di'monds wear.

The ballad is in the Pepys Collection, iv. 253, entitled, " The Beggar's Delight, as it was sung at the Theatre Royal : printed for P. Brooksby," &c. No song of the King of Poland is known.

## I OFTEN FOR MY JENNY STROVE.

*The Banquet of Music,* 1689; *Apollo's Banquet,* 1690; *The Dancing Master,* 1695, &c.; *Pills to purge Melancholy,* all editions ; *The Jovial Crew,* and other Ballad Operas.

If thou wouldst but think on me, And now for-sake thy cru-el-ty,

I for ev-er could be, should be, would be Join'd to none, but on-ly thee.

When first I saw thy lovely charms,
I kiss'd thee, wish'd thee in my arms ;
I often vow'd and still protest
'Tis Joan alone that I love best.

I have gotten twenty pounds,
My father's house, and all his grounds,
And for ever would be, should be, could be
Join'd with none, but only thee.

These words are from *The Banquet of Music*, which is described on the title as consisting of " Songs sung at the Court and Theatres."

There are many black-letter ballads to the tune in the Pepys, Roxburghe, and Douce Collections, such as " The Love-sick Serving Man ; showing how he was wounded with the charms of a young lady, and did not dare to reveal his mind " (Roxburghe, ii. 299) ; " The old Miser slighted " (Roxburghe, ii. 387), &c.

One of the ballads sung to the air, entitled *Cupid's Revenge*, is almost a paraphrase of *King Cophetua and The Beggar Maid*—alluded to by Shakespeare, and reprinted by Percy in the *Reliques*. " Cupid's Revenge " is contained in *Old Ballads*, i. 138, 8vo, 1723, and in Evans *Old Ballads*, ii. 361, 1810. It commences thus :—

> " A king once reign'd beyond the seas,
>   As we in ancient stories find,
>  Whom no fair face could ever please :
>   He cared not for womankind.
>  He despis'd the sweetest beauty,
>   And the greatest fortune too ;
>  At length he married to a beggar,
>   See what Cupid's dart can do," &c.

## THE RANT.

*Apollo's Banquet;* and many Ballad Operas.

This is the tune to which the song "How happy could I be with either," in *The Beggar's Opera*, was sung. It originally belonged to a ballad called "The Jolly Gentleman's Frolick; or, The City Ramble," &c., a copy of which was in Mr. Payne Collier's Collection.

Another ballad in the Bagford Collection, called "The Ranting Rambler," &c., and a third, in the Roxburghe Collection, ii. 359, called "Mark Noble's Frolick," &c., were also sung to it.

About fifty years later, we find it quoted in Ritson's *Bishoprick Garland, or Durham Minstrel*, as the tune of a song of "The Hareskin"; commencing :—

> "Come hither, attend to my ditty,
> All you that delight in a gun,
> And, if you'll be silent a minute,
> I'll tell you a rare piece of fun.
>     Fal, lal," &c.

And Mr. J. H. Dixon prints a ballad entitled "Saddle to Rags," which is still sung in the North of England, to the same air. The last will be found in *Ballads and Songs of the Peasantry of England*, 8vo, 1846.

## LADIES OF LONDON.

*The Dancing Master*, 1690, &c.; *Apollo's Banquet*, 1690; *Pills to purge Melancholy*, all editions; many of the Ballad Operas.

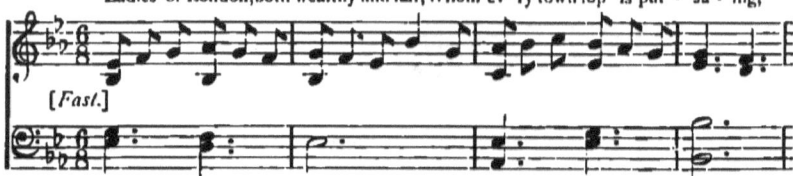

Ladies of London, both wealthy and fair, Whom ev-'ry town fop is pur-su-ing,

[*Fast.*]

Pray of yourselves and your purses take care, The great-est de-ceit lies in woo-ing.

From the first rank of the *beaux esprits*, Their vi-ces I here will dis-cov-er,

Down to the bas-est me-chan-ic de-gree, That so you may choose out a lov-er.

A black-letter copy of the ballad is in the Roxburghe Collection, ii. 5, printed for J. Back, on London Bridge, and entitled "Advice to the Ladies of London in the choice of their husbands: to an excellent new Court tune."

The following were also sung to it:—

" Advice to the Ladies of London to forsake their fantastical topknots, since they are become so common with Billingsgate women, and the wenches that cry kitchen stuff," &c.; " to the tune of *Ye Ladies of London*"; beginning :—

"Now you young females that follow the mode."

"The Country Maiden's Lamentation"; beginning :—

"There came up a lass from a country town,
  Intending to live in the city,
In steeple-crown hat, and a paragon gown,
  Who thought herself wondrous pretty.
Her petticoat serge; her stockings were green," &c.

The two last are in the Douce Collection. In the Roxburghe, ii. 101, is :—

"A country gentleman came up to town,
  To taste the delights of the city,
Who had to his servant a jocular clown,
  Accounted to be very witty," &c.

There are several more in the same volume (see pp. 97, 444, 519, and 530), and in the Pepys Collection iv. 16 :—" The Witty Maid of the West; or, The Miller well thrash'd by Robin the Plowman : for which service he received a sum of money, which bought a ring and paid for the marriage betwixt him and his beloved Nancy. Tune of *Ladies of London.*" It begins :—

"William the miller, who liv'd in the West."

## JAMES THE SECOND'S MARCH.

*The Dancing Master*, 1690, there called "The Garter"; in later editions, "King James's March, or the Garter."

## THE NORTHUMBERLAND BAGPIPES.

*Pills to purge Melancholy*, ii. 136, 1700; *Apollo's Banquet*, 1693, there called "A New Dance in the play of the *Marriage Hater Match'd*"; Wright's *Dancing Master*, vol. i., p. 10, there called "The Boyan."

M.

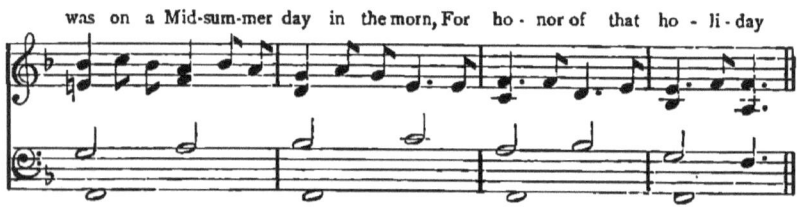

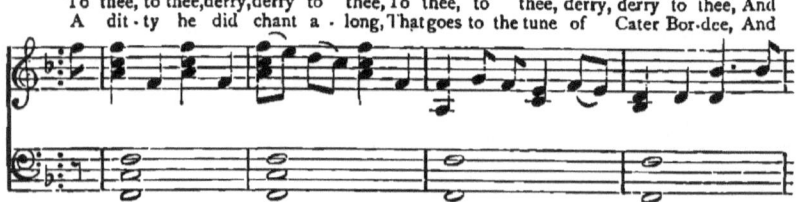

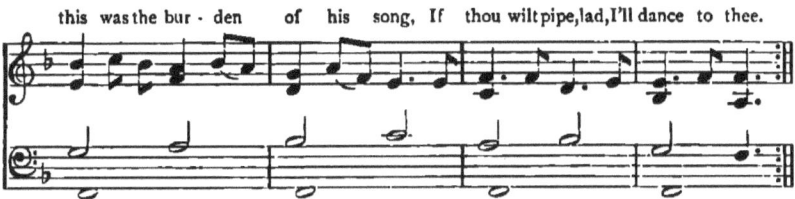

| And whilst this harmony he did make, | Her bongrace was of wended straw, |
| A country damsel from the town, | From the sun's beams her face to free, |
| A basket on her arm she had, | And thus she began, when she him saw, |
| A gathering rushes on the down : | *If thou wilt pipe, lad, I'll dance to thee*, &c. |

These are the words printed with the tune in *Pills to purge Melancholy*. They are also to be found in the Roxburghe Collection, ii. 363, and Bagford, 643, m. 10, p. 159, with the title "The Merry Bagpipes: the pleasant pastime betwixt a jolly shepherd and a country damsel on a Midsummer's day in the morning. To the tune of *March, boys*," &c. Licensed according to order, and printed by C. Bates, next door to the Crown Tavern in West Smithfield.

The dance version of the tune, from *Apollo's Banquet*, is as follows:—

## WILLY WAS SO BLITHE A LAD.

Playford's *Choice Ayres*, there called "A Northern Song"; *Youth's Delight on the Flagelet*, 1697, there called "Billy was as blyth a lad."

## THE BAFFLED KNIGHT.

*Youth's Delight on the Flagelet*, 9th and 11th ed., 1697.

For continuation of the words, see Percy's *Reliques of Ancient Poetry*. A similar ballad which might be sung to the tune is in the Roxburghe Collection, i. 306, entitled "The Politick Maid; or—

> "A dainty new ditty, both pleasant and witty,
> Wherein you may see the Maid's policie."

"To a pleasant new tune." Subscribed R[ichard] C[limsall], and "printed for Thomas Lambert, at the signe of the Horse-shoe, in Smithfield."

> "There was a Knight was wine-drunk,
>   As he rode on the way,
> And there he spied a bonny lasse
>   Among the cocks of hay.
> *Sing, loud whistle in the wind,*
>   *Blow merry, merry;*
> *Up and down in yonder dale,*
>   *With hey tro, nonney, nonney.'*

## THE LATER POPULAR MUSIC.

In Roxburghe, ii. 578, will also be found "The West Country Lawyer; or, The Witty Maid's Good Fortune," &c.: "to the tune of *The Baffled Knight*"; commencing :—

> "A youthful lawyer, fine and gay,
>   Was riding unto the city,
> Who met a damsel on the way,
>   Right beautiful, fair, and witty.
>
> 'Good morrow, then, the lawyer cried,
>   'I prithee, where art thou going?
> Quoth she, 'To yonder meadow's side,
>   My father is there a mowing,'" &c.

Another upon a similar subject is contained in *Pills to purge Melancholy*, iii., 1707, or v., 1719; and in *A Complete Collection of Old and New English and Scotch Songs*, 8vo, 1735. It has a separate tune (see *Pills*), and is in stanzas of eight lines, commencing :—

> "There was a Knight, and he was young."

## AYE, MARRY, AND THANK YE TOO.

*Youth's Delight on the Flagelet*, 1697; *Silvia*, 1731, and *Robin Hood*, 1730 (Ballad Operas.)
M.

[*Moderate.*]

Nothing is known of the original ballad (of which this title was the burden), except its first line: "I live in the town of Lynn"; but a continuation of it (with a somewhat similar tune) will be found in *Pills to purge Melancholy*, iii. 131, 1707; commencing :—

> "I am the young lass of Lynn,
> Who often said, 'Thank you too.'"

## THE LATER POPULAR MUSIC. 71

Many ballads were sung to the tune, among others :—
In the Pepys Collection, iv. 65, "The May Morning Ramble; or, Robin and Kate, &c.: tune of *I marry and thank ye too.*" It begins :—

"Kind Robin he met young Kate."

In the same collection, v. 3, p. 79, "Nell's Humble Petition; or, The Maiden's kind and courteous Courtship to honest John the Joyner, whose love she earnestly desired: to the tune of *I marry and thank ye too.*" It begins :—

"There was an old maid of late."

Also in the Roxburghe Collection, ii. 290, and Evans, i. 85, "The London Lass's Lamentation; or, Her fear she should never be married," which begins thus :—

"Alas! I am in a rage,
   And bitterly weep and cry;
Because I'm nineteen years of age,
   Yet cannot be married, not I.

Mine eyes do like fountains flow,
   As I on my pillow lie,
There's none know what I undergo,
   Yet cannot be married, not I.

My father is grey and old,
   And, surely, ere long will die,
And though he'll leave me all his gold,
   Yet cannot be married, not I.

In silks I am still array'd,
   And ev'ry new fashion buy,
Because I'm so loth to die an old maid,
   Yet cannot be married, not I.

The gold which I have in store
I value no more than clay,
I'd give it all, and ten times more,
So I might be married to-day."

## RED BULL.

*The Dancing Master*, 1698, &c.; *Apollo's Banquet for the Treble Violin*, there called "The Damsell's Dance."

This tune is named after the Red Bull Playhouse, which formerly stood in St. John Street, Clerkenwell. It was in use throughout the reigns of James I. and Charles I., and perhaps before. At the Restoration, the King's actors, under Thomas Killigrew, played there until they removed to the new theatre in Drury Lane; and when Davenant produced his *Playhouse to be Let*, in 1663, it was entirely abandoned.—(See Collier's *Annals of the Stage*.)

In the Roxburghe Collection, i. 246, is a ballad entitled "A Mad Kind of Wooing; or, A Dialogue between Will the simple and Nan the subtle, with their loving agreement: to the tune of *The new Dance at the Red Bull Playhouse*." It is in black-letter, printed for the assigns of T. Symcocke, whose patent for "printing of paper and parchment on the one side" was granted in 1620, and assigned in the same year. Another copy of the ballad will be found in the Pepys Collection, i. 276, "printed for H[enry] G[osson] on London Bridge."

## GREENWICH PARK, OR COME SWEET LASS.

With the first title in *The Dancing Master*, 1698; with the second in *The Beggars Opera*, and in *Pills to purge Melancholy*, all editions.

On our green
The loons are sporting,
Piping, courting,
On our green
The blithest lads are seen ;
There, all day,
Our lasses dance and play,
And every one is gay,
But I, when you're away.
   How can I
Have any pleasure
While my treasure
   Is not by?
The rural harmony

I'll not mind,
But, captive like, confin'd,
I lie in shades behind,
'Cause Moggy proves unkind.

There is none
That can delight me,
If you slight me ;
All alone,
I ever make my moan.
Life's a pain,
Since by your coy disdain,
Like an unhappy swain,
I sigh and weep in vain.

This ballad is in the Pepys Collection, vol. v., 263, entitled " An excellent new Scotch Song, call'd Jockey's Complaint for his beloved Moggy, together with Moggy's kind Answer, as it was lately sung in a new play at the Royal Theatre."

74    THE LATER POPULAR MUSIC.

It was also printed in *The Compleat Academy of Complements*, 1685 ; and in several other collections.

A ballad, also in the Pepys Collection, vol. v., 275, called " Perjured Billy," &c., was directed to be sung to this tune.

## MAD MOLL, OR THE VIRGIN QUEEN,
### OR
## YELLOW STOCKINGS.

With the first title in *The Dancing Master*, 1698, &c., and another version with the second title, 1703, &c. ; with the third title in Wright's *North Country Frisks*, 1713, and in the *Boarding School* (Ballad Opera), 1733.

The above is the earliest version of the tune, known as *Mad Moll*.

Swift's song, " O my Kitten," was written to the version called *The Virgin Queen*.

## THE DEVIL'S PROGRESS.

*Pills to purge Melancholy*, 1699, 1707, 1719.

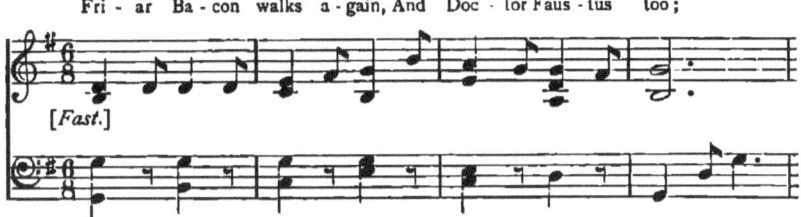

Why think you that he laugh'd?
  Forsooth he came from court;
And there, amongst the gallants,
  Had spied such pretty sport:
There was such cunning juggling,
  And ladies grown so proud—
Huggle, duggle, &c.

With that into the City
  Away the devil went,
To view the merchants' dealings
  It was his full intent;
And there along the brave Exchange
  He crept into the crowd—
Huggle, duggle, &c.

He went into the City,
  To see all there was well;
Their scales were false, their weights were
  Their conscience fit for hell; [light,
And "bad men" chosen Magistrates,
  And Puritans allow'd—
Huggle, duggle, &c.

With that into the country
  Away the devil goeth,
For there is all plain dealing,
  And that the devil knoweth:
But the rich man reaps the gains,
  For which the poor man plough'd—
Huggle, duggle, &c.

With that the devil in haste,
  Took post away to hell,
And told his fellow furies
  That all on earth was well;
That falsehood there did flourish,
  Plain-dealing was in a cloud—
Huggle, duggle, ha, ha, ha,
  The devils laugh'd aloud.

The ballad of *The Devil's Progress on Earth, or Huggle-duggle*, is contained in *Pills to purge Melancholy*, vol. i, 1699 and 1707; or vol. iii., 1719. The words of the first stanza are very imperfectly printed in all editions. Three or four words have here been added or altered from conjecture. "Airing" stands "Alridg," in the *Pills;* the word after "Pluto" is deficient; "And many a goblin more" is here changed to "*O'er* many a goblin *crew*," because a rhyme is required to "too."

In the *Rump Songs*, i. 101, ed. 1662, and in *Collection of Loyal Songs written against the Rump Parliament*, i. 50, is "The Sense of the House; or, The Reason why those Members who are the Remnant of the Two Families of Parliament cannot consent to Peace, or an Accommodation: to the tune of *The New-England Psalm, Huggle-duggle, ho, ho, ho, the Devil he laugh'd aloud*." It begins:—

"Come, come, beloved Londoners, fie, fie, you shame us all!
Your rising up for peace will make the close Committee fall:
I wonder you dare ask for that, which they must needs deny,—
There's thirty swear they'll have no peace, and bid me tell you why."

## BARTHOLOMEW FAIR, or THE DUTCHWOMAN'S JIGG.

*Pills to purge Melancholy,* vol. i., 1699-1714, vol. iii., 1719; *The Dancing Master,* 1695, &c.; *The Quakers,* and other Ballad Operas.

Ad - zooks! che's went the o - ther day to Lon - don town, In

[*Moderate.*]

Smith-field such gaz - ing, such thrust - ing and squeez-ing, was nev - er known.

A zit - ty of wood! some volks do call it Bar - tle - dom Fair, But

che's zure nought but kings and queens live there.

In gold and zilver, zilk and velvet, each was drest,
A Lord in his zatin was busy a prating among the rest,
But one in blue jacket did come, whome some do Andrew call,
Adsheart, talk'd woundy wittily to them all.

At last, cutzooks, he made such sport, I laugh'd aloud,
The rogue being fluster'd, he flung me a custard, amidst the croud.
The volk vell a laughing at me; and then the vezen said,
" Be zure, Ralph, give it to Doll, the dairy maid."

These words are from *Pills to purge Melancholy*; but they are also to be found in ballad form in the Pepys Collection, v. 438, entitled "Roger in amaize; or, The Countryman's Ramble through Bartholomew Fair: tune of *The Dutchwoman's Jigg*," &c.

## TOBACCO'S BUT AN INDIAN WEED.

*Pills to purge Melancholy*, 1699, &c.

In *The Marrow of Complements*, 1654, p. 176, is a poem entitled "Meditations on Tobacco," with the initials G[eorge] W[ither], which is as follows:—

"Why should we so much despise
So good and wholesome an exercise
As, early and late, to meditate?
  Thus think, and drink tobacco.

The earthen pipe, so lily white,
Shews that thou art a mortal wight;
Even such—and gone with a small touch:
  Thus think, and drink tobacco.

And when the smoke ascends on high,
Think on the worldly vanity
Of worldly stuff—'tis gone with a puff:
  Thus think, and drink tobacco.

And when the pipe is foul within,
Think how the soul's defil'd with sin—
To purge with fire it doth require:
  Thus think, and drink tobacco.

Lastly, the ashes left behind
May daily shew, to move the mind,
That to ashes and dust return we must:
  Thus think, and drink tobacco."

About 1670 we find several copies of Wither's song, but the first stanza changed in all, besides other minor variations. In *Merry Drollery Complete*, 1661, it commences: "Tobacco, that is withered quite." On broadsides, bearing date 1670, and having the tune at the top, the first line is, "The Indian weed withered quite."

In 1699 it appeared in *Pills to purge Melancholy*, with the tune, thus:—

" Tobacco's but an Indian weed,
  Grows green at morn, cut down at eve,
  It shows our decay, we are but clay :
    Think of this when you smoke tobacco.

The pipe, that is so lily white,
  Wherein so many take delight,
  Is broke with a touch—man's life is such :
    Think of this when you smoke tobacco.

The pipe, that is so foul within,
  Shews how man's soul is stain'd with sin,
  And then the fire it doth require :
    Think of this when you smoke tobacco.

The ashes that are left behind
  Do serve to put us all in mind
  That unto dust return we must :
    Think of this when you smoke tobacco.

The smoke, that does so high ascend,
  Shews us man's life must have an end.
  The vapour's gone—man's life is done :
    Think of this when you smoke tobacco."

After the *Pills*, it was printed with alterations, and the addition of a very inferior second part, by the Rev. Ralph Erskine, a minister of the Scotch Church, in his *Gospel Sonnets*. This is the "Smoking Spiritualised," which by various means, and in various publications, has been kept alive almost to the present day.

## THERE WAS AN OLD WOMAN LIV'D UNDER A HILL.

*Pills to purge Melancholy*, all editions ; *The Jovial Crew*, and other Ballad Operas.

The miller he kiss'd her ; away she went,
Sing trolly, lolly, lolly, lolly lo ;
The maid was well pleas'd, and the miller content.
Oh ho ! Oh ho ! Oh ho ! was it so?

He danc'd and he sung, while the mill went clack.
Sing trolly, lolly, lolly, lolly lo ;
And he cherish'd his heart with a cup of old sack,
Oh ho ! Oh ho ! Oh ho ! did he so?

These are the words set to the tune in *The Jovial Crew.*

## THE COBBLER'S HORNPIPE.

*The Dancing Master* of 1701, and subsequent editions ; also in vol. i. of Walsh's *Compleat Country Dancing Master.*

## LAY THE BENT TO THE BONNY BROOM.

*Pills to purge Melancholy.*

# THE LATER POPULAR MUSIC. 81

There was a knight of noble worth, *Lay the bent, &c.*
Who also lived in the North, *Fa, la, &c.*
This knight, of courage stout and brave,
A wife he did desire to have ;
He knocked at the lady's gate,
One evening when it was late.
The eldest sister let him in,
And pinn'd the door with a silver pin, &c.

This ballad and tune are contained in the second volume of the early editions of *Pills to purge Melancholy*, and in the fourth volume of the later.

Copies of the ballad are also in the Pepys, iii. 19, Douce, 169, and Halliwell Collections, No. 253. It is entitled "A noble riddle wisely expounded ; or, The Maid's answer to the Knight's three questions : —

' She, with her excellent wit and civil carriage,
Won a young knight to joyn with her in marriage.
This gallant couple now are man and wife,
And she with him doth lead a pleasant life.'

" The tune is *Lay the bent to the Bonny Broom.*"

The copy in the Halliwell Collection was printed for F. Coles, T. Vere, and W. Gilbertson, who all commenced publishing before the Restoration. It is in W. Thackeray's list of ballads, and the copy in the Douce Collection was printed by Thomas Norris, at the Looking-glass on London Bridge. The original is probably of early date.

## AN OLD WOMAN POOR AND BLIND.

*Pills to purge Melancholy*, all editions ; *The Village Opera*, 1729 ; *The Fashionable Lady*, 1730.

[*Moderate.*]

The ballad was printed by W. Thackeray, in the reign of Charles II., and subsequently by Playford and his successors, and is to be found in all the editions of *Pills to purge Melancholy*, with the tune.

There are several other ballads to the air in the *Pills*, and among them, one on " The Cries of London," beginning, " Come, buy my greens and flowers fine ;" and a second, " The Crafty Cracks of East Smithfield." The latter has the burden of " I'm plundered of all my gold."

In the Bagford Collection of Ballads are the following :—

"The Toothless Bride," &c.: " to the tune of *An Old Woman poor and blind.*"

"The Deptford Plumb Cake; or, The Four Merry Wives: tune, *An Old Woman poor and blind.*"

In *A Pill to purge State Melancholy*, v. ii., 1718, "Here's a health to great Eugene;" a song on Prince Eugene's routing the Turks, to the same air.

In the Roxburghe and other collections, "A Dialogue between Jack and his Mother: tune of *Old Woman poor and blind.*"

## SHACKLEY-HAY.

Skene MS. (late 17th century).

84  THE LATER POPULAR MUSIC.

| But all in vain she did complain, | No, no, quoth she, I thee deny, |
|---|---|

But all in vain she did complain,
For nothing could him move,
Till wind did turn him back again,
And brought him to his love.
When she saw him thus turn'd by fate,
She turn'd her love to mortal hate ;
Then weeping, to her he did say,
I'll live with thee at Shackley-hay.

No, no, quoth she, I thee deny,
My love thou once did scorn,
And my prayers wouldst not hear,
But left me here forlorn.
And now, being turn'd by fate of wind,
Thou thinkst to win me to thy mind ;
Go, go, farewell ! I thee deny,
Thou shalt not live at Shackley-hay.

Copies of this ballad, "to the tune of *Shackley-hay,*" are in the Pepys Collection, i. 350 ; in the Roxburghe, i. 436 and 472 ; the Bagford, fol. 75 ; and it is reprinted in Evans' *Old Ballads,* i. 50.

In the Pepys Collection, i. 344, is a ballad of "Leander's Love to Hero : to the tune of *Shackley-hay,*" beginning :—

"Two famous lovers once there was.

In *Westminster Drollery,* 1671 and 1674, "A Song of the Declensions : the tune is *Shackle de hay,*" and the same, with two others, in *Grammatical Drollery,* by W. H. (Captain Hicks), 1682.

In the Roxburghe Collection, ii. 244, and the Douce Collection, p. 109, is "The Knitter's Job ; or, The Earnest Suitor of Walton Town to a Fair Maid, with her modest answers, and conclusion of their intents : to the tune of *Shackley-hey.*" It commences thus :—

"Within the town of Walton fair
A lovely lass did dwell ;
Both carding, spinning, knitting yarn,
She could do all full well."


## THE SPANISH LADY.

The Skene MS.; *The Quaker's Opera,* 1728, &c.

The words are to be found in *The Garland of Good-will*, and in several of the celebrated collections of ballads; also in Percy's *Reliques*, series ii., book 2; and in the folio MS., iii. 395.

Percy says, "This beautiful old ballad most probably took its rise from one of those descents made on the Spanish coasts in the time of Queen Elizabeth: and, in all likelihood, from the taking of the city of Cadiz (called by our sailors, corruptly, Cales), on June 21, 1596, under the command of the Lord Howard, admiral, and of the Earl of Essex, general."

The ballad of "The Spanish Ladies Love" was entered at Stationers' Hall to William White, 11th June, 1603. It is quoted in *Cupid's Whirligig*, 1616, and in Brome's *Northern Lasse*, and is parodied in Rowley's *A Match at Midnight*, 1633. In Mrs. Behn's comedy, *The Rovers*, one of the characters is constantly singing the ballad. In the Douce Collection, ii. 210 and 212, there are two copies, the one "to a pleasant new tune"; the other (which is of later date) to the tune of *Flying Fame;* but could not be sung to that air. In the same volume, p. 254, is "The Westminster Wedding, or Carlton's Epithalamium" (dated 1663): to the tune of *The Spanish Lady*. It commences thus:—

"Will you hear a German Princess,
How she chous'd an English Lord," &c.

## I HAVE BUT A MARK A YEAR.

*Pills to purge Melancholy*, ii. 116, 1700, &c.

The copy of this ballad in the Roxburghe Collection, i. 122, is entitled "A Fair Portion for a Fair Maid ; or,—

> 'The thrifty maid of Worcestershire,
> Who lives at London for a mark a year ;
> This mark was her old mother's gift,
> She teaches all maids how to thrift.'"

A shortened version is to be found with the tune, and also in *The Aviary*, p. 332.

In the Roxburghe Collection, i. 328, and reprinted in Collier's *Roxburghe Ballads*, is a ballad, "The Praise of Nothing : to the tune of *I have but a marke a yeare.*"

## OLD NOLL'S JIG.

*The Dancing Master*, 1701, &c.

A song called "When once Master Love gets into your Head" was sung to this tune.

## PORTSMOUTH.

*The Dancing Master,* 11th edition, &c

[*Moderate.*]

The words to this tune (probably a ballad) have not been discovered.

## TURN AGAIN, WHITTINGTON.[1]

*Pills to purge Melancholy,* iii. 40, 1707; Hawkins' Transcripts.

[1] The story of the poor stranger, whose ill fortune is suddenly reversed by the performances of his cat, is of Eastern origin; but it is also to be found in Arlotto's Italian novels, published about 1483. It is not easy to see why it should have been adopted in this country as the legend of a Lord Mayor who was himself a knight's son, a Londoner, and probably never poor. It should, however, be remembered that the ordinary coasting vessel, more particularly a collier, of from four to six hundred tons, was formerly called a cat; and a cat of this kind is much more likely than *Felis domestica* to have been instrumental in making a Lord Mayor's fortune.

The earliest notice I have observed of *Turn again, Whittington*, as a tune (if a mere change upon bells may come under that denomination), is in Shirley's *Constant Maid*, act ii., sc. 2, 4to, 1640, where the niece says:—

> "Faith, how many churches do you mean to build
> Before you die? six bells in every steeple,
> And let them all go to the *city tune*,
> *Turn again, Whittington*—who, they say,
> Grew rich, and let his land out for nine lives,
> 'Cause all came in by a cat."

Mr. Burn points out various earlier notices of Whittington and his cat, as in *Eastward Hoe* (printed in 1605), where Touchstone assures Golding he hopes to see him reckoned one of the worthies of the city of London, "when the famous fable of Whittington and his puss shall be forgotten."

The ballad was entered at Stationers' Hall a few months later than a drama on the same subject. The following extracts are from the registers of the Company. On February 8, 1604-5, entered to Tho. Pavier, "The History of Richard Whittington, of his lowe birthe, his great fortune, as yt was plaied by the Prynce's Servants"; and on July 6 (1605) to Jo. Wright, "a ballad called The wondrous Lyfe and memorable Death of Sir Ri: Whittington now sometyme Lo: Maior of the honorable Citie of London."

Wright was the printer. The ballad (or another on the same subject) was written by Richard Johnson, author of *The Seven Champions of Christendom*, &c., and is contained in his *Crowne Garland of Goulden Roses*, 1612. Copies are also in the Douce Collection, fol. 103; in *Old Ballads*, i. 132, 1723; in Evans' Collection, ii. 325, 1810; and in Mackay's *Songs of the London Prentices and Trades*, &c.

In *Pills to purge Melancholy* the tune is called *Turn again, Whittington;* in Hawkins' transcripts of virginal music *The Bells of Osney;* and as the ballad of "Sir Richard Whittington" was to be sung to the tune of *Dainty, come thou to me*, this may be another name for the same. A fourth seems to be *Whittington's Bells*, for Ward, in *The London Spy*, says, "he'd rather hear an old barber ring *Whittington's Bells* upon the cittern" than all the music-houses then afforded.

## FELTON'S GAVOT, OR FAREWELL, MANCHESTER.

This tune was composed in the early part of the last century by the Rev. Wm. Felton, prebendary of Hereford. It formed a part of one of his Concertos, and was afterwards published with variations as Felton's Gavot. It is said to have been played by the troops of Charles Stuart on quitting Manchester in December, 1745; also when the unfortunate Manchester youth, Dawson, was executed in 1746. About the same period some words were written to it, entitled "A Song made on the Peace," a copy of which, bearing the prefix of "Farewell, Manchester," and printed with the music, is in the British Museum (G. 307, p. 230). The song of "Farewell, Manchester," is, in all probability, irrecoverably lost.

## ADMIRAL BENBOW

*Dale's Collection*, i. 68.

The first we came up with was a brigantine sloop,
And we ask'd if the others were big as they look'd ;
But turning to windward as near as we could lie,
We found there were ten men of war cruising by.

Oh ! we drew our squadron in very nice line,
And boldly we fought them for full four hours' time ;
But the day being spent, boys, and the night coming on,
We let them alone till the very next morn.

The very next morning the engagement prov'd hot,
And brave Admiral Benbow receiv'd a chain shot ;
And when he was wounded, to his merry men he did say,
"Take me up in your arms, boys, and carry me away."

Oh the guns they did rattle, and the bullets did fly,
But Admiral Benbow for help would not cry ;
"Take me down to the cockpit, there is ease for my smarts,
If my merry men see me it will sure break their hearts."

The very next morning, by break of the day,
They hoisted their topsails, and so bore away ;
We bore to Port Royal, where the people flock'd much
To see Admiral Benbow carried to Kingston Church.

Come all you brave fellows, wherever you've been,
Let us drink to the health of our King and our Queen,
And another good health to the girls that we know,
And a third in remembrance of brave Admiral Benbow.

The subject of this ballad is mentioned in Evelyn's Diary, under the date of January, 1702-3. "News of Vice-Admiral Benbow's conflict with the French fleet in the West Indies, in which he gallantly behaved himself, and was wounded, and would have had extraordinary success, had not four of his men-of-war stood spectators without coming to his assistance ; for this, two of their commanders were tried by a council of war and executed ; a third was condemned to perpetual imprisonment, loss of pay, and incapacity to serve in future. The fourth died."

I suspect that this was originally a much longer ballad, and that the last stanza was substituted for the remaining verses at a later date. The story is only half told, all notice of the treachery of the four captains is omitted, as well as of their trial, and the death of the Admiral. Perhaps the balled was thus curtailed to be sung upon the stage.

The words are contained in a collection of song books formerly belonging to Ritson.

## BENBOW, THE BROTHER TAR.

The Broadsides with music.

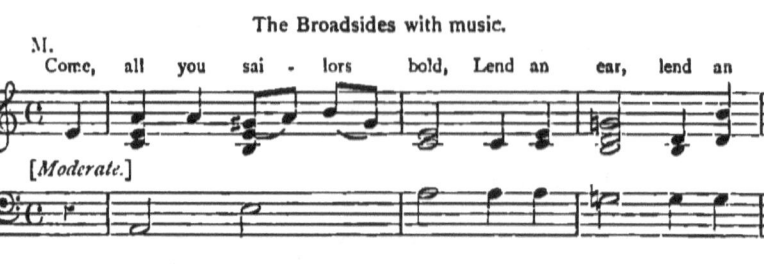

[1] Admiral Benbow was called "the brother tar" because he rose from before the mast to the rank of Admiral. His father was Colonel John Benbow, a Shropshire gentleman and loyal Cavalier, who distinguished himself at the battle of Worcester, and was there taken prisoner. At the Restoration he could obtain no better post than one of subordinate rank in the Tower of London at a salary of eighty pounds a year, and left his family penniless.

## THE LATER POPULAR MUSIC. 95

Brave Benbow he set sail
For to fight, for to fight,
Brave Benbow he set sail for to fight :
Brave Benbow he set sail,
With a fine and pleasant gale,
But his Captains they turn'd tail
In a fright, in a fright.

Says Kirby unto Wade,
" I will run, I will run,"
Says Kirby unto Wade, " I will run :
I value not disgrace,
Nor the losing of my place,
My enemies I'll not face
With a gun, with a gun."

'Twas the Ruby and Noah's Ark
Fought the French, fought the French,
'Twas the Ruby and Noah's Ark fought
And there was ten in all,      [the French :
Poor souls they fought them all,
They valued them not at all,
Nor their noise, nor their noise.

It was our Admiral's lot
With a chain shot, with a chain shot,
It was our Admiral's lot, with a chain shot.
Our Admiral lost his legs,
And to his men he begs,
" Fight on, my boys," he says,
" 'Tis my lot, 'tis my lot."

While the surgeon dress'd his wounds,
Thus he said, thus he said,
While the surgeon dress'd his wounds, thus
" Let my cradle now in haste    [he said :
On the quarter-deck he plac'd,
That my enemies I may face
Till I'm dead, till I'm dead."

And there bold Benbow lay
Crying out, crying out,
And there bold Benbow lay, crying out
" Let us tack about once more,
We'll drive them to their own shore,
I value not half a score,
Nor their noise, nor their noise."

This is taken from a broadside printed with the tune in the first half of the last century ; but the words are evidently much corrupted. For instance, the line, " Nor their noise," at the end of the fourth stanza, cannot be correct, as it ought to rhyme with " French," and the same words are again substituted, at the end of the last stanza, for a line that should rhyme with " crying out."

Mr. Halliwell prints the words in *Early Naval Ballads of England*, from a broadside published at Salisbury, by Fowler, a noted ballad-printer of the last century, but the same corruptions are in both copies.

## THE ROAST BEEF OF OLD ENGLAND.

Walsh's *British Musical Miscellany*, N.D. ; *The Universal Musician*, N.D.

When mighty roast beef was the Englishman's food,
It ennobled our hearts, and enriched our blood ;
Our soldiers were brave, and our courtiers were good.
    Oh, the roast beef of old England!
    And oh, for old England's roast beef!

But since we have learn'd from effeminate France
To eat their ragouts, as well as to dance,
We are fed up with nothing but vain complaisance.
    Oh, the roast beef, &c.

Our fathers of old were robust, stout, and strong,
And kept open house, with good cheer all day long,
Which made their plump tenants rejoice in this song.
    Oh, the roast beef, &c.

When good Queen Elizabeth sat on the throne,
Ere coffee and tea, and such slip-slops were known,
The world was in terror if e'en she did frown.
    Oh, the roast beef, &c.

In *those* days, if fleets did presume on the main,
They seldom or never return'd back again ;
As witness the vaunting Armada of Spain.
    Oh, the roast beef, &c.

Oh, then we had stomachs to eat and to fight,
And when wrongs were cooking, to set ourselves right ;
But now we're a—hm !—I could, but good night.
    Oh, the roast beef, &c.

The words and air of this song are by R. Leveridge.

## THREE TRAVELLERS.

*Pills to purge Melancholy*, vi. 177.

There were three tra-vel-lers, tra-vel-lers three, With a
[*Fast.*]

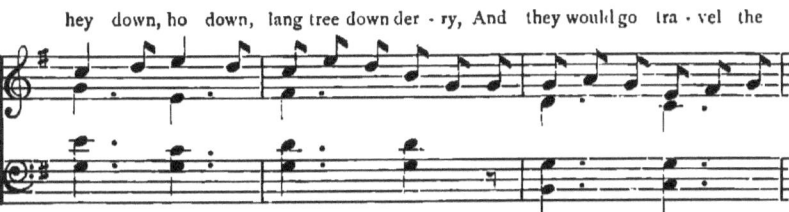

hey down, ho down, lang tree down der-ry, And they would go tra-vel the

North Coun-try, Without ev-er a sti-ver of mon-ey.

A copy of the ballad in the Bagford Collection (643, m. 9, p. 88) is entitled "The Jovial Companions; or, The Merry Travellers, who paid their shot where ever they came, without ever a stiver of money: to *an excellent North-country tune.*" Printed by C. Bates, at the Sun and Bible in Pye Corner. It is also contained in *Pills to purge Melancholy*, vi. 177.

In a Collection of Satirical Songs by the Earl of Rochester (Harl. MSS., No. 6,913) is "A new ditty to an old tune of *Three Travellers*," beginning :—

> "I'll shew you the Captains of Aubrey Vere,
> With a hey ho, langled down dilly;
> Fit Captains to serve with so noble a peer,
> Who has *never a penny of money.*"

## GOOD MORROW, GOSSIP JOAN.

*Pills to purge Melancholy*, vi. 315; *The Beggars' Opera*, and several others.

My sparrow's flown away,
  And will no more come to me ;
I've broke a glass to-day,
  The price will quite undo me,
        Gossip Joan.

I've lost a *Harry* groat
  Was left me by my granny ;
I cannot find it out,
  I've search'd in ev'ry cranny,
        Gossip Joan.

I've lost my wedding ring,
  That was made of silver gilded ;
I had drink would please a king,
  But that my cat had spill'd it,
        Gossip Joan.

My pocket is cut off,
  That was full of sugar-candy ;
I cannot stop my cough
  Without a gill of brandy,
        Gossip Joan.

    Let's to the ale-house go,
      And wash down all our sorrow,
    My griefs you there shall know,
      And we'll meet again to-morrow,
            Gossip Joan.

Another song to the same tune, called "Happy Dick," is in Watt's *Musical Miscellany*, iv. 36, and in the *Vocal Miscellany*, 1734, vol i.

## CUPID'S COURTESIE, OR I AM SO DEEP IN LOVE.

*Pills to purge Melancholy*, vi. 43.

> "Little boy, tell me why thou art here diving;
> Art thou some runaway, and hast no biding?"
> "I am no runaway; Venus, my mother,
> She gave me leave to play, when I came hither."
> "Little boy, go with me, and be my servant;
> I will take care to see for thy preferment."
> "If I with thee should go, Venus would chide me,
> And take away my bow, and never abide me," &c.

Copies of this ballad are in the Roxburghe Collection, ii. 58; Pepys, iii. 219; and in the Douce Collection, p. 27. It was licensed to Coles, Wright, Vere, and Gilbertson, March 13, 1655.

The copy in the Roxburghe Collection may be dated as of the reign of Charles II., being "printed by and for W. O[nley], for A[lexander] M[ilbourne], and sold by the booksellers"; but Mr. Payne Collier, who reprints it in his *Book of Roxburghe Ballads*, p. 80, mentions "a manuscript copy, dated 1595," as still extant. The ballad is entitled "*Cupid's Courtesie;* or, The young Gallant foil'd at his own weapon," &c.: "to a most pleasant *Northern tune.*"

In another volume of the Douce Collection (p. 264) is "The Young Man's Vindication against The Virgin's Complaint: tune of *The Virgin's Complaint, or Cupid's Courtesie*"; commencing:—

> "Sweet virgin, hath disdain
> Mov'd you to passion,—
> Ne'er to love man again,
> But for the fashion?" &c.

Upon this copy a former possessor has pencilled against the name of the tune, "*I am so deep in love,*" but this is only another name for *Cupid's Courtesie*, derived from a ballad in the Pepys Collection, iii. 218, called "The Maiden's Complaint against Young Men's Unkindness":—

> "Of young men's falshood she doth much complain,
> Resolving never to love man again;
> Experience tells her men love but for fashion—
> What makes her rail against them in such passion?"

To the tune of *Cupid's Courtesie*. The first line is, "I am so deep in love."

In the Roxburghe Collection, ii. 24, is "The Bashful Virgin; or, The Secret Lover: tune of *I am so deep in love*, or *Little Boy*," &c.

## JOAN TO THE MAYPOLE.

*Pills to purge Melancholy*, 1707 and 1719.

This ballad is in the Roxburghe Collection, ii. 354, and Douce Collection, p. 152. It is entitled "May-day Country Mirth; or, The

Young Lads' and Lasses' Innocent Recreation, which is to be prized before courtly pomp and pastime: to an excellent new tune." The title of the Pepys copy, iv. 244, is "Rural Recreations; or, The Young Men and Maids' Merriment at their Dancing round a Country May-pole: to an excellent new tune." Printed by W. Thackeray. Dr. Rimbault, in his *Little Book of Songs and Ballads, gathered from Ancient Music-books*, prints a version "from a MS. volume of old songs and music, formerly in the possession of the Rev. H. J. Todd, dated 1630." The same is in Evans' *Old Ballads*, i. 245, 1810. Another version will be found with the tune in *Pills to purge Melancholy*, ii. 145, 1707, or iv. 145, 1719, with many more stanzas. Also in *Pills*, iii. 25, 1707, a song by D'Urfey called "The Disappointment," to the tune.

One of Richard Brathwaite's *Shepherds' Tales* (printed in 1621) is "The Shepherd's Holiday, reduced in apt measures to Hobbinall's Galliard, or *John to the Maypole*" (see the Rev. T. Corser's *Collectanea Anglo Poetica*, part ii., p. 366).

In *Mock Songs and Joking Poems*, 1675, is "A Mock to Joan to the Maypole away let us run: and to that tune." It begins:—

"Tom, to the tavern away let us run,
The wine will waste and soon be gone."

## ST. GEORGE FOR ENGLAND.

*Pills to purge Melancholy*, 1707 and 1719, &c.

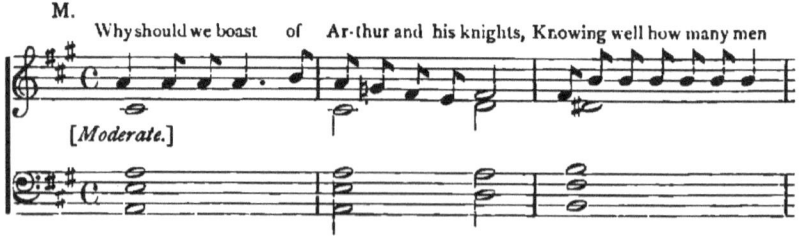

## THE LATER POPULAR MUSIC. 103

There are black-letter copies of this ballad in the Pepys and Bagford Collections.

The ballad in the Pepys Collection, i. 87, is entitled "Saint George's Commendation to all Souldiers; or, Saint George's Alarum to all that profess martiall discipline, with a memoriall of the Worthies who have been borne so high on the wings of Fame for their brave adventures, as they cannot be buried in the pit of oblivion: to *a pleasant new tune.*" It was "imprinted at London, by W. W.," in 1612, and is the copy from

which Percy printed, in his *Reliques of Ancient Poetry.* It begins:
" Why do we boast of Arthur and his Knightes."

In Antony Wood's Collection, at Oxford, No, 401, there is a modernization of this ballad, entitled :—

> "St. George for England, and St. Dennis for France,
> O hony soite qui mal y pance :

to *an excellent new tune."*—(Wood's Ballads, ii. 118.) It is subscribed S. S., and " printed for W. Gilbertson, in Giltspur Street" ; from which it may be dated about 1659.

It is also in *An Antidote to Melancholy*, 1661 ; in part ii. of *Merry Drollery Complete*, 1661 and 1670 ; *Wit and Drollery*, 1682 ; *Pills to purge Melancholy*, 1707 and 1719, &c.

The ballad is one of those offered for sale by the ballad-singer in Ben Jonson's comedy of *Bartholomew Fair.*

Pepys, in his Diary, tells us of " reading a ridiculous ballad, made in praise of the Duke of Albemarle, to the tune of *St. George*—the tune being printed too " ; and adds, " I observe that people have great encouragement to make ballads of him, of this kind. There are so many, that hereafter he will sound like Guy of Warwick."—(March 6, 1667.)

Fielding, in his novel of *Tom Jones*, makes *St. George he was for England* one of Squire Western's favourite tunes.

In 180 *Loyal Songs*, 1685 and 1694, there is a " A new song on the instalment of Sir John Moor, Lord Mayor of London : tune, *St. George for England* " ; and in *Pills to purge Melancholy*, iii. 20, 1707, " A new ballad of King Edward and Jane Shore," to the same.

## THE FADING.

*Pills to purge Melancholy*, 1707.

"Fading" was the burden of a popular Irish song, and gave the name to a dance, frequently noticed by our old dramatists.—(See Giffard's *Jonson*, vii., p. 240.)

> "See you yon motion? not the old fa-ding,
> Nor Captain Pod, nor yet the Eltham thing."
> —(*The Silent Woman*, act v., sc. 1.)

There are ballads to the tune in the Roxburghe Collection, ii. 16; and Pepys, i. 224, and iii. 248 and 287 ; and songs in *Sportive Wit*, &c., 1656, and *Pills to purge Melancholy*, i. 90, 1707.

## COME LET US PREPARE.

Watts's *Musical Miscellany*, iii. 72 ; *British Melody*, &c., 1739 ; *The Dancing Master*, vol. iii. ; *The Village Opera*, and several others.

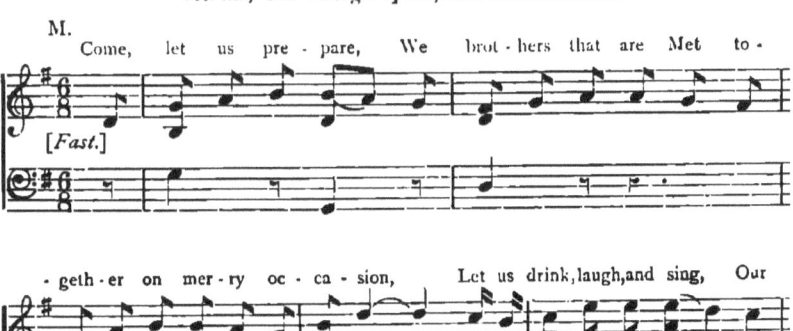

| | |
|---|---|
| The world is in pain | Antiquity's pride |
| Our secret to gain, | We have on our side, |
| But still let them wonder and gaze on, | It makes each man just in his station; |
| Till they're shown the light | There's nought but what's good, |
| They'll ne'er know the right | To be understood |
| Word or sign of an accepted Mason. | By a free and an accepted Mason. |
| | |
| 'Tis this, and 'tis that, | We're true and sincere, |
| They cannot tell what, | We're just to the fair, |
| Why so many great men of the nation | They'll trust us on ev'ry occasion; |
| Should aprons put on, | No mortal can more |
| To make themselves one | The ladies adore |
| With a free and an accepted Mason. | Than a free and an accepted Mason. |
| | |
| Great kings, dukes, and lords, | Then join hand in hand, |
| Have laid by their swords, | To each other firm stand, |
| This our myst'ry to put a good grace on, | Let's be merry and put a bright face on; |
| And ne'er been asham'd | What mortal can boast |
| To hear themselves nam'd | So noble a toast |
| With a free and an accepted Mason. | As a free and an accepted Mason? |

In *The Gentleman's Magazine* for October, 1731, the first stanza is printed as "A Health, by Mr. Birkhead." It seems to be there quoted from "The Constitutions of the Freemasons, by the Rev. James Anderson, A.M., one of the worshipful Masters."

There are several versions of the tune. One in *Pills to purge Melancholy*, ii. 230, 1719, has a second part, but that, being almost a repetition of the first, taken an octave higher, is out of the compass of ordinary voices, and has therefore been generally rejected.

In *A Complete Collection of Old and New English and Scotch Songs*, ii. 172, 1735, the name is given as "Ye Commons and Peers," but Leveridge composed another tune to those words.

In "The Musical Mason, or Free Mason's Pocket Companion, being a Collection of Songs used in all Lodges: to which are added The Free Mason's March and Ode," 8vo, 1790, this is entitled "The Enter'd Apprentice's Song."

Among the songs sung to this tune is one contained in *The True Loyalist, or Chevalier's Favourite*, which begins:—

"Here's a health to the King,
Whose right 'tis to reign,
Tho' supplanted by a race of usurpers ;
To our shame and disgrace
That mean, spurious race
Are ador'd by flagitious disturbers."

And another, called "The Progress to the Bath," in *The Merry Musician*, vol. i.

## HERE'S A HEALTH TO ALL HONEST MEN.

*The Dancing Master*, vol. ii., 1718 and 1728 ; Watts's *Musical Miscellany*, ii. 142, 1730 ; the ballad opera of *The Jovial Crew ; The Convivial Songster*, 1782, &c.

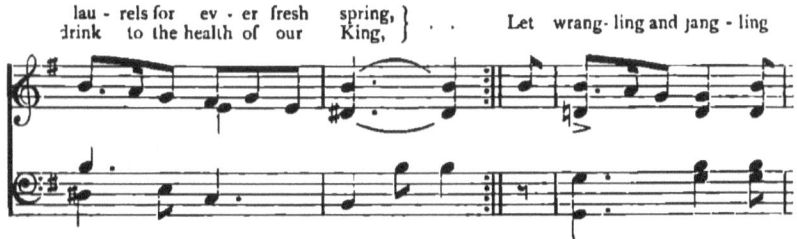

## THE LATER POPULAR MUSIC.

To-ry nor Whig, With your par-ties look big, Here's a health to all honest men.

'Tis not owning a whimsical name
That will prove a man loyal or just ;
Let him fight for his country's fame,
Be impartial at home, if in trust :
'Tis this that proves him an honest soul,
His health we'll drink in a brimful bowl ;
Then leave off all debate,
No confusion create :
Here's a health to all honest men !

When a company's honestly met,
With intent to be jolly and gay,
Their drooping souls for to whet,
And drown the fatigues of the day,
What madness it is thus to dispute,

When neither side can his man confute !
When you've said what you dare,
You're but just where you were :
Here's a health to all honest men !

Then agree, ye true Britons, agree ;
Never quarrel about a nickname ;
Let your enemies tremblingly see
That an Englishman's always the same.
For our king and our church, our laws and right,
Let's lay by all feuds, and straight unite.
O then, why care a fig
Who's a Tory or Whig ?
Here's a health to all honest men !

## THE HAPPY CLOWN.

*The Dancing Master*, vol. ii., 1718 and 1728 ; Walsh's *Compleat Country Dancing Master*, i. 13 ; many Ballad Operas, and Half-sheets.

## THE LATER POPULAR MUSIC.

Sometimes the air is entitled "The Happy Clown," and sometimes "Walpole; or, The Happy Clown"; but it is now more generally known by the words, "I'm like a skiff on ocean toss'd," in *The Beggars' Opera*.

The song of "The Happy Clown," commencing, "One evening, having lost my way," was written by Mr. Burkhead. In *The Convivial Songster*, "As one bright sultry summer's day" is printed to the tune, and those words may be older than any of the above.

### COME JOLLY BACCHUS, OR CHARLES OF SWEDEN.

*The Dancing Master*, vols. ii. and iii. ; Walsh's *Lady's Banquet;* many of the Ballad Operas.

M.
2. Let none at cares of life re - pine, To des troy our plea - sure :
1. Come, jol- ly Bac - chus, god of wine, Crown this night with plea - sure;

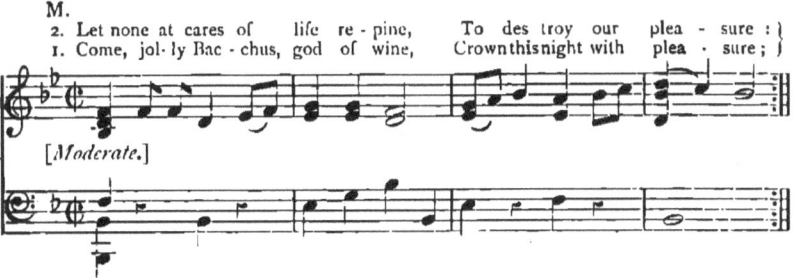

[*Moderate.*]

Fill up the migh - ty spark-ling bowl, That ev - 'ry true and loy - al soul,

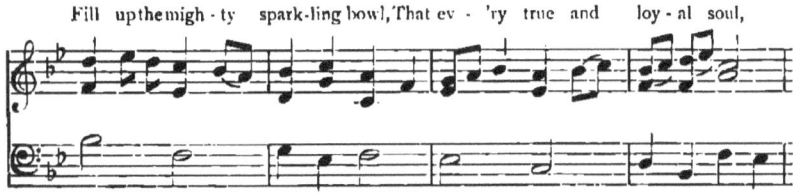

Let lovers whine, and statesmen think,
  Always void of pleasure ;
And let the miser hug his chink,
  Destitute of pleasure :
But we like sons of mirth and bliss,
  Obtain the height of happiness,
Whilst brimmers flow with juice like this,
  In the midst of pleasure.

Thus, mighty Bacchus, shalt thou be
  Guardian to our treasure ;
That under thy protection we
  May enjoy new pleasure ;
And as the hours glide away,
  We'll in thy name invoke their stay,
And sing thy praises, that we may
  Live and die in pleasure !

In the second volume of *The Dancing Master* this tune is called "Frisky Jenny ; or, The tenth of June ;" in the third volume it is again printed under the title of "The Constant Lover." In Walsh's *Lady's Banquet* it appears as "The Swedes Dance at the new Playhouse"; in *The Devil to pay*, and *The Rival Milliners ; or, The Humours of Covent Garden*, as "Charles of Sweden"; and in *The Beggar's Wedding* as "Glorious first of August." The song of "Come, jolly Bacchus," by the name of which it is now best known, was written to the tune in *The Devil to pay*

The following ballads and songs were also sung to it :—

1. On the taking of Portobello in 1739, entitled "English Courage display'd ; or, Brave news from Admiral Vernon : to the tune of *Charles of Sweden*." Contained in *The Careless Bachelor's Garland*. It is a long ballad of eleven stanzas, commencing thus :—

  "Come, loyal Britons, all rejoice, with joyful acclamation,
  And join with one united voice upon this just occasion.
  To Admiral Vernon drink a health, likewise to each brave fellow
  Who with that noble Admiral was at the taking of Portobello."

2. "A song to the tune of *Come, jolly Bacchus, god of wine.*" Two stanzas.

"Come, gallant Vernon, come, and prove
  How firm your friends are here, Sir ;
Supported by the Public Love,
  You will have nought to fear, Sir.

Soon shall mistaken boasters know
  That we can still some virtue shew,
Resolved to ward corruption's blow,
  And check its swift career, Sir."

3. "A new song made on board the Salamander, Privateer."

  "Come, let's drink a health to George our King,
  And all his brave Commanders :
  Another glass let us then toss off,
  To the valiant Salamander," &c.

## THE MOUSE-TRAP, OR OLD HOB.

*The Dancing Master*, vol. ii.; *Pills to purge Melancholy*, i. 250, 1719; Watts's *Musical Miscellany*, 1731; *The Beggars' Opera*, and many others

The words of this song are by D'Urfey, "made to a comical tune in *The Country Wake*," a play written by Doggett, and printed in 1696.

## THE MAN OF KENT.

*Pills to purge Melancholy*, vol. ii., p. 5, 1719; *The Quakers*, and other Ballad Operas.

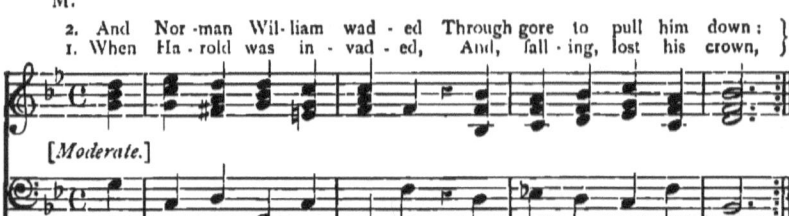

2. And Nor-man Wil-liam wad-ed Through gore to pull him down;
1. When Ha-rold was in-vad-ed, And, fall-ing, lost his crown,

[*Moderate.*]

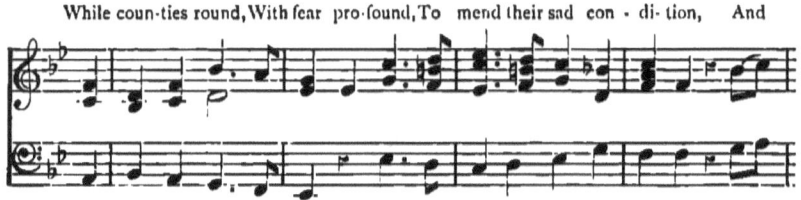

While coun-ties round, With fear pro-found, To mend their sad con-di-tion, And

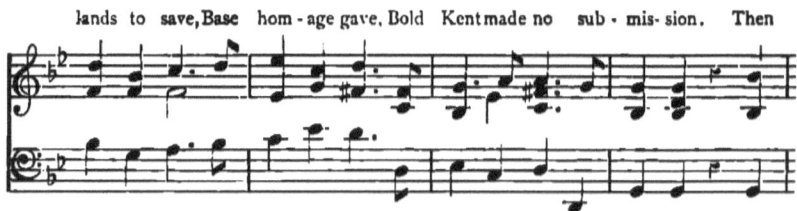

lands to save, Base hom-age gave, Bold Kent made no sub-mis-sion. Then

sing in praise of the Men of Kent, So loy-al, brave, and free; Of

Bri-ton's race, If one sur-pass, A Man of Kent is he.

The hardy stout freeholders,
　That knew the tyrant near,
In girdles, and on shoulders,
　A grove of oaks did bear :

Whom when he saw in battle draw,
　And thought how he might need 'em;
He turn'd his arms, allow'd their terms,
　Complete with noble freedom.

The song of "The Man of Kent" is by D'Urfey, and the tune by Leveridge, composer of "The Roast Beef of Old England," "Black-ey'd Susan," &c.

D'Urfey wrote a second song to the same air for his play of *Masaniello*, and Leveridge, who was a bass singer, sang it on the stage.

The latter is in praise of fishing, commencing, "Of all the world's enjoyments," and has the following burden :—

"Then who a jolly fisherman, a fisherman will be,
　His throat must wet, just like his net,
　To keep out cold at sea."

## MAY FAIR.

*Pills to purge Melancholy,* i. 169, 1719 ; *The Beggars' Opera,* 1728 ; *The Grub Street Opera,* and others ; also in some editions of *The Dancing Master.*

The tune is sometimes called *O Jenny, Jenny, where hast thou been?* from a song by D'Urfey, entitled "The Willoughby Whim."

## COME LASSES AND LADS.

*Pills to purge Melancholy*, vol. iii., 1719.

Strike up, says Wat,—agreed, says Matt,
   And I prithee, fiddler, play ;
Content, says Hodge, and so says Madge,
   For this is a holiday.
Then every lad did doff
   His hat unto his lass,
And every girl did curtsey, curtsey,
   Curtsey on the grass.

Begin, says Hal,—aye, aye, says Mall,
   We'll lead up *Packington's Pound;*
No, no, says Noll, and so says Doll,
   We'll first have *Sellenger's Round.*
Then every man began
   To foot it round about,
And every girl did jet it, jet it,
   Jet it in and out.

You're out, says Dick,—not I, says Nick,
   'Twas the fiddler play'd it wrong ;
'Tis true, says Hugh, and so says Sue,
   And so says every one.
The fiddler then began
   To play the tune again,
And every girl did trip it, trip it,
   Trip it to the men.

Let's kiss, says Jane,—content, says Nan,
   And so says every she ;
How many ? says Batt,—why, three, says
   For that's a maiden's fee.   [Matt,
The men, instead of three,
   Did give them half a score ;
The maids in kindness, kindness, kindness,
   Gave 'em as many more.

Then, after an hour, they went to a bow'r,
   And play'd for ale and cakes ;
And kisses too,—until they were due
   The lasses held the stakes.
The girls did then begin
   To quarrel with the men,
And bade them take their kisses back,
   And give them their own again.

Now there they did stay the whole of the
   And tired the fiddler quite   [day,
With dancing and play, without any pay,
   From morning until night.
They told the fiddler then
   They'd pay him for his play,
And each a twopence, twopence, twopence,
   Gave him, and went away.

[Good night, says Harry,—good night, says Mary ;
   Good night, says Dolly to John :
Good night, says Sue, to her sweetheart, Hugh ;
   Good night, says everyone.
Some walk'd, and some did run ;
   Some loiter'd on the way,
And bound themselves by kisses twelve
   To meet the next holiday.]

The earliest copy I have found of this still popular ballad is in *Westminster Drollery*, part ii., 1672, entitled "The Rural Dance about the May-pole : the tune, the first Figure-Dance at Mr. Young's Ball, in May, '71." The copy in *Tixall Poetry*, 4to, 1813, taken from an old manuscript, contains a final stanza not to be found in *Westminster Drollery*.

## POOR ROBIN'S MAGGOT.

*The Dancing Master*, vol. ii.; *Pills to purge Melancholy*, 1719; *The Beggars' Opera*, and many others.

## SALLY IN OUR ALLEY.

Carey's *Musical Century*, ii. 32 ; in Walsh's *Dancing Master*, vol. ii., 1719 ; in *The Beggars' Opera; The Devil to pay; The Fashionable Lady; The Merry Cobbler; Love in a Riddle; The Rival Milliners;* and numerous Half-sheet Songs.

Her father he makes cabbage-nets,
  And through the streets does cry them;
Her mother she sells laces long,
  To such as please to buy them:
But sure such folks could ne'er beget
  So sweet a girl as Sally;
She is the darling of my heart,
  And lives in our alley.

When she is by, I leave my work,
  I love her so sincerely;
My master comes, like any Turk,
  And bangs me most severely:
But let him bang, long as he will,
  I'll bear it all for Sally;
She is the darling of my heart,
  And lives in our alley.

Of all the days are in the week,
  I dearly love but one day,
And that's the day that comes betwixt
  A Saturday and Monday:
For then I'm dress'd in all my best,
  To walk abroad with Sally;
She is the darling of my heart,
  And lives in our alley.

My master carries me to church,
  And often I am blamed,
Because I leave him in the lurch,
  Soon as the text is named:
I leave the church in sermon time,
  And slink away to Sally;
She is the darling of my heart,
  And lives in our alley.

When Christmas comes about again,
  Oh, then I shall have money;
I'll hoard it up, and box and all
  I'll give unto my honey:
I would it were ten thousand pounds,
  I'd give it all to Sally;
She is the darling of my heart,
  And lives in our alley.

My master and the neighbours all
  Make game of me and Sally,
And but for her I'd better be
  A slave, and row a galley:
But when my sev'n long years are out,
  Oh, then I'll marry Sally,
And then how happily we'll live—
  But not in our alley.[1]

Among the songs printed to Carey's tune are the following:—

1. "Sally's Lamentation; or, The Answer to Sally"; beginning:—

  "What pity 'tis so bright a thought
    Should e'er become so common;
  At ev'ry corner brought to naught
    By ev'ry bawling woman.
  I little thought, when you began
    To write of charming Sally,
  That ev'ry brat would sing so soon,
    'She lives in our alley.'"

---

[1] The following is Carey's account of the origin of his song:—"A vulgar error having prevailed among many persons, who imagine Sally Salisbury the subject of this ballad, the author begs leave to undeceive and assure them it has not the least allusion to her, he being a stranger to her very name at the time this song was composed: for, as innocence and virtue were ever the boundaries of his muse, so, in this little poem, he had no other view than to set forth the beauty of a chaste and disinterested passion, even in the lowest class of human life. The real occasion was this: A shoemaker's 'prentice, making holiday with his sweetheart, treated her with a sight of Bedlam, the puppet shows, the flying-chairs, and all the elegancies of Moorfields, from whence proceeding to the farthing-pye-house, he gave her a collation of buns, cheesecakes, gammon of bacon, stuffed beef, and bottled ale, through all which scenes the author dodged them. Charmed with the simplicity of their courtship, he drew from what he had witnessed this little sketch of nature; but, being then young and obscure, he was very much ridiculed by some of his acquaintance for this performance, which nevertheless made its way into the polite world, and amply recompensed him by the applause of the *divine Addison*, who was pleased more than once to mention it with approbation."

2. "Sally in our Alley to Billy in Piccadilly; with proper graces to the tune."

"Of all the lads that are so smart
There's none I love like Billy;
He is the darling of my heart,
And he lives in Piccadilly," &c.

3. "Sally in her own cloaths"; beginning:—

"Of all the mauxes in the land
There's none I hate like Sally."

4. "Sally rivall'd by Country Molly"; commencing:—

"Since Sally's charms so long have been
The theme of court and city,
Pray, give me leave to raise the song
And praise a girl more pretty."

5. "Blowzabel. A Song"; commences:—

"Of Anna's charms let others tell,
Of bright Eliza's beauty;
My song shall be of Blowzabel,
To sing of her's my duty."

6. "As Damon late with Chloe sat."

About 1760 Carey's tune was superseded by on older ballad tune, and though both were concurrently in favour for some time, Carey's tune eventually gave way to the older one, which is now the only one sung to the words.—(See vol. i., p. 300.) The two tunes curiously resemble each other in the closes; and this may have led, first to their confusion, and afterwards to the adoption of the one which was most easy to sing.

## CEASE YOUR FUNNING.

*The Beggars' Opera; The Fashionable Lady*, 1730.

'Tis most cer-tain, But their flirt-ing, Wo-men oft have en-vy shown;

Pleas'd to ru-in O-thers' woo-ing; Nev-er hap-py in their own.

These are the words given in *The Beggars' Opera*. The tune is not named, but as all the other tunes contained in the opera were older than the work itself, the same may be presumed of this also.

## AN OLD WOMAN CLOTHED IN GRAY.

Henry Carey's *Musical Century*, vol. ii ; *The Beggars' Opera*, 1728 ; *Humours of the Court*, 1732 ; Walsh's *Dancing Master*, there called " Unconstant Roger."

M.

[*Moderate.*]

A copy of "An Old Woman clothed in Gray," in Dr. Burney's Collection of songs, with music (Brit. Mus.), has a manuscript date of 1662. In *Old Ballads*, ii. 230, 1726, the song of "An old Woman clothed in Gray" is to the tune of *Kind Husband and Imperious Wife*. The song of "The Kind Husband but Imperious Wife" is contained in *Westminster Drollery*, 1671, and in *Wit and Drollery*, 1682, but the tune is not named in either. Here, therefore, the pedigree halts. It should be traceable higher, for I am convinced that words such as those of "Kind Husband" never had music *composed* for them. They are a dialogue between a man and his wife, and commence :—

> " Wife, prithee come give me thy hand now,
> And sit thee down by me ;
> There's never a man in the land now
> Shall be more loving to thee."

Another version of the tune is known as *Let Oliver now be forgotten*, from a song by D'Urfey, printed in his *New Collection of Songs and Poems*, 8vo, p. 52, 1683, entitled "Tony : a Ballad made occasionally by reading a late speech made by a noble Peer." The tune is not printed there, but is given with the words in 180 *Loyal Songs*, 1685 and 1694, and in *Pills to purge Melancholy*, ii. 283, 1719. It was also known as *How unhappy is Phillis in love*, from some song now lost. The tune, without words, is in Salter's *Genteel Companion for the Recorder*, 1683, and in Lady Catherine Boyd's MS. Lyra Viol Book, lately in the possession of Mr. A. Blaikie. Many political ballads were written to it under one or other of these names, especially about the year 1680. For instance, in Mr. Halliwell's Collection, Cheetham Library, are at fol. 171: "An excellent new ballad of the plotting head : to the tune of *How unhappy is Phillis in love ;* or, *Let Oliver now be forgotten*." Printed for R. Moor, 1681. At fol. 243, " Tony's Lamentation ; or, Potapski's City Case, being his last farewell to the consecrated Whigs : the tune is, *Let Oliver now be forgotten*," 1682. In 180 *Loyal Songs*, " The Conspiracy ; or, The discovery of *the fanatick plot*, 1684 ; and in Mat. Taubman's *Heroic Poem and choice Songs and Medleyes on the times*, " Philander," fol. 1682.

## THE COUNTRY GARDEN, or THE VICAR OF BRAY.

With the first title in *The Quakers' Opera*, and many others.

When royal James possess'd the crown,
And popery grew in fashion,
The penal laws I hooted down,
And read the Declaration :
The church of Rome I found would fit
Full well my constitution ;
And I had been a Jesuit,
But for the Revolution.
    And this is law, &c.

When William was our King declar'd
To ease the nation's grievance ;
With this new wind about I steer'd,
And swore to him allegiance :
Old principles I did revoke,
Set conscience at a distance ;
Passive obedience was a joke,
A jest was non-resistance.
    And this is law, &c.

When royal Anne became our queen,
The church of England's glory,
Another face of things was seen,
And I became a tory :
Occasional conformists base,
I blam'd their moderation ;
And thought the church in danger was,
By such prevarication.
    And this is law, &c.

When George in pudding-time came o'er,
And moderate men look'd big, sir,
My principles I chang'd once more,
And so became a whig, sir ;
And thus preferment I procur'd
From our new faith's-defender ;
And almost ev'ry day abjur'd
The Pope and the Pretender.
    And this is law, &c.

Th' illustrious house of Hanover,
And Protestant succession,
To these I do allegiance swear—
While they can keep possession :
For in my faith and loyalty,
I never more will falter,
And George my lawful king shall be—
Until the times do alter.
    And this is law, &c.

Nichols in his *Select Poems* says that the song of the Vicar of Bray " was written by a soldier in Colonel Fuller's troop of Dragoons, in the reign of George I."

## THE BUDGEON IT IS A DELICATE TRADE.

*The Quakers' Opera*, 1728; *The Fashionable Lady; Love in a Village.*

The song to this tune is contained in *The Canting Academy*, 2nd ed., 1674; in *A Warning to Housekeepers*, &c., 1676; in *The Triumph of Wit*, &c.; and in *A New Canting Dictionary*, &c., "with a complete collection of songs in the canting dialect," 1725. The first verse is as follows :—

"The budgeon it is a delicate trade,
   And a delicate trade of fame,
For when that we have bit the bloe,
   We carry away the game.

But if the cully nab us, and
   The lurries from us take,
O then he rubs us to the whit,
   Though we are not worth a make."

The "budge" would appear to be the particular kind of thief that slips into houses in the dark, to steal cloaks and other articles near the door.

In 1762 the song sung to it in *Love in a Village* was the well known—*There was a jolly Miller* :—

> "There was a jolly miller once liv'd on the river Dee ;
> He danc'd and he sang from morn till night, no lark so blithe as he.
> And this the burden of his song for ever us'd to be—
> I care for nobody, no, not I, if nobody cares for me," &c.

THE LATER POPULAR MUSIC.   125

On a half-sheet with music published by Walsh in "The Vocal Musical Mask: a collection of English songs never before printed, set to music by Mr. Lampè, Mr. Howard," &c., is "A Sailor's Song sung by Mr. Beard in the Fair," which is to this tune. It begins :—

> "What cheer, my honest messmates ;
> You're welcome all on shore,
> We've done our duty bravely,
> And ready to do more," &c.

## SWEET NELLY MY HEART'S DELIGHT.

*The Merry Musician; or, A Cure for the Spleen*, ii. 78 ; Watts's *Musical Miscellany*, i. 130, 1729 ; the Broadsides, &c.

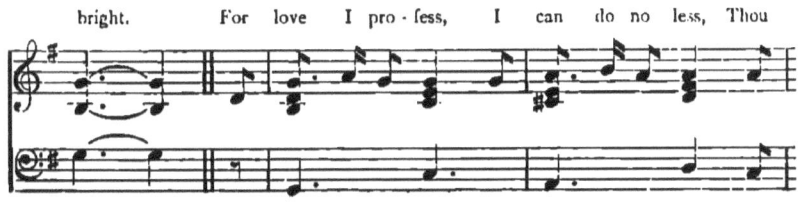

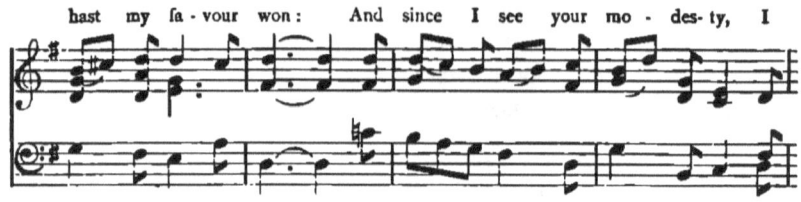

*She.* No! I am a lady gay,
It is very well known I may
Have men of renown,
In country or town ;
So, Roger, without delay,
Court Bridget or Sue,
Kate, Nancy, or Prue,
Their loves will soon be won ;
But don't you dare
To speak me fair,
As if I were
At my last pray'r,
To marry a farmer's son.

*He.* My father has riches in store,
Two hundred a year and more ;
Besides sheep and cows,
Carts, harrows, and ploughs,
His age is above three-score ;
And when he does die,
Then merrily I

Shall have what he has won ;
Both land and kine,
All shall be thine,
If thou'lt incline
And wilt be mine,
And marry a farmer's son.

*She.* A fig for your cattle and corn !
Your proffer'd love I scorn.
'Tis known very well
My name it is Nell,
And you're but a bumpkin born.

*He.*   Well, since it is so,
Away I will go,
And I hope no harm is done.
Farewell ! adieu !
I hope to woo
As good as you,
And win her, too,
Though I'm but a farmer's son, &c.

There is also in the Pepys Collection, v. 216 :—" The Conquer'd Lady ; or, The Country Wooing between Robin, the rich Farmer's Son, and Madam Nelly, a Nobleman's Daughter, as they met together by chance in the town of Bath : tune of *The Milking Pail.*" It begins :—

"Young Nelly, my heart's delight."

London : Printed for J. Blare, at the Looking Glass on London Bridge.

## AS DOWN IN THE MEADOWS.

*The Merry Musician,* ii. 129 ; Watts's *Musical Miscellany,* i. 62 ; *Polly,* 1729, and many other Ballad Operas ; the Broadsides.

M.

2. Her age, I am sure, it was scarce-ly fif-teen, And she on her head wore a
1. As down in the mea-dows I chanc'd for to pass, O there I be-held a young

[*Moderate.*]

gar-land of green.
beau-ti-ful lass, } Her lips were like ru-bies, and as for her eyes, They

spark-led like dia-monds, or stars in the skies ; And then, O her voice, it was

charm-ing and clear, As sad-ly she sung for the loss of her dear.

## THE COUNTRY COURTSHIP.

*The Dancing Master*, vol. iii ; Walsh's *New Country Dancing Master*, &c.

The "song entitled The Country Courtship, beginning, 'Honest Sir, give me thy hand,'" was entered at Stationers' Hall, to John Back, March 31, 1688.

## GRIM KING OF THE GHOSTS.

Watts' *Musical Miscellany*, i. 26, 1729; *The Beggars' Opera*, &c.

Black-letter copies of this ballad are to be found in the Bagford, the Pepys, the Douce, and the Roxburghe Collections. It is usually entitled "The Lunatick Lover; or, The Young Man's call to Grim King of the Ghosts for cure: to *an excellent new tune.*" Percy reprinted it in his

*Reliques of Ancient Poetry*, and Ritson in his *Select Collection of English Songs*; the first stanza will therefore suffice.

> "Grim King of the Ghosts! make haste,
> And bring hither all your train:
> See how the pale moon does waste,
> And just now is in the wane.
>
> Come, you night hags, with all your charms,
> And revelling witches, away,
> And hug me close in your arms;
> To you my respects I'll pay."

Among the ballads sung to the tune are the following :—

1. "The Father's Wholesome Admonition: to the tune of *Grim King of the Ghosts*."—(See Roxburghe Collection, ii. 165.)

2. "The Subjects' Satisfaction: being a new song of the proclaiming King William and Queen Mary, the 13th of this instant February, to the great joy and comfort of the whole kingdom: to the tune of *Grim King of the Ghosts; or, Hail to the myrtle shades*."—(See Roxburghe Collection, ii. 437.)

3. "The Protestant's Joy; or, An excellent new song on the glorious Coronation of King William and Queen Mary, which in much triumph was celebrated at Westminster on the 11th of this instant April: tune of *Grim King of the Ghosts; or, Hail to the myrtle shades*." This has a woodcut intended to represent the King and Queen seated on the throne. —(See Bagford Collection, 643, m. 10, p. 172, Brit. Mus.) "Printed for J. Deacon, in Guiltspur Street."

To this tune Rowe composed his well-known song, "Colin's Complaint," which begins :—

> "Despairing beside a clear stream,
> A shepherd forsaken was laid," &c.

Which has been reprinted in Ritson's *English Songs*, and in many other collections and which has been so often parodied.

## FAIR ROSALIND.

*Mercurius Musicus*, 1735; Watts' *Musical Miscellany*, ii. 176, 1729, there called "The Jilt"; *The Convivial Songster*, 1780, &c.

Wretched, and only wretched, he,
To whom that lot shall fall;
For, if her heart aright I see,
She means to please them all.

## FAIR MARGARET AND SWEET WILLIAM.

Watts' *Musical Miscellany*, ii. 84, 1729; *The Village Opera*, 1729.

| I see no harm by you, Margaret, | Then down she laid her ivory comb, |

I see no harm by you, Margaret,
  And you see none by me ;
Before to-morrow at eight o' the clock
  A rich wedding you shall see.

Fair Margaret sat in her bower-window,
  Combing her yellow hair ;   [bride,
There she spied sweet William and his
  As they were a riding near.

Then down she laid her ivory comb,
  And braided her hair in twain ;
She went alive out of her bower,
  But ne'er came alive in't again.

When day was gone, and night was come,
  And all men fast asleep,
Then came the spirit of fair Marg'ret,
  And stood at William's feet, &c.

Percy says: "This seems to be the old song quoted in Fletcher's *Knight of the Burning Pestle*, acts ii. and iii., although the six lines there preserved are somewhat different from those in the ballad as it stands at present. The lines preserved in the play are this distich:—

> "You are no love for me, Margaret,
> I am no love for you ;"

and the following stanza:—

> "When all was grown to dark midnight,
> And all were fast asleep,
> In came Margaret's grimly ghost,
> And stood at William's feet."

Copies of this ballad are in the Douce Collection, fol. 72 ; Roxburghe, iii. 338 and 342 ; and in the Collection of Mr. George Daniel ; also in Percy's *Reliques of Ancient Poetry*.

The copy in the Douce Collection is entitled "Fair Margaret's Misfortune ; or, Sweet William's frightful dreams on his wedding night : with the sudden death and burial of those noble lovers. To an excellent new tune."

THE LATER POPULAR MUSIC. 133

## PHILLIDA FLOUTS ME.

Watt's *Musical Miscellany*, ii. 132, 1729; *The Quaker's Opera*, 1728, &c.

At the fair t'other day,
As she pass'd by me,
She look'd another way,
And would not spy me.
I woo'd her for to dine,
But could not get her;

Dick had her to the Vine,
He might intreat her.
With Daniel she did dance,
On me she would not glance;
Oh, thrice unhappy chance!
Phillida flouts me, &c.

The ballad of "Phillida flouts me" is in the Roxburghe Collection ii. 142, and Ritson printed the words in his *Ancient Songs*, from a copy in *The Theatre of Compliments; or, New Academy*, 1689, but did not discover the tune.

In *The Crown Garland of Golden Roses*, 1612, is "A short and sweet sonnet made by one of the Maides of Honor upon the death of Queene Elizabeth, which she sowed upon a sampler in red silke: to a new tune, or *Phillida flouts me;*" beginning:—

"Gone is Elizabeth,
Whom we have lov'd so dear," &c.

Patrick Carey also wrote a ballad to the tune of *Phillida flouts me;* beginning :—

> "Ned ! she that likes thee now,
> Next week will leave thee !" ·

It is contained in his " Trivial Poems and Triolets, written in obedience to Mrs. Tomkin's commands, 20th August, 1651." In Walton's *Angler,* 1653, the Milkwoman asks, "What song was it, I pray? Was it *Come, Shepherds, deck your heads,* or *As at noon Dulcina rested,* or *Phillida flouts me?*"

Another name for the tune is *Love one another.* This is derived from a song called "The Protestant Exhortation," where it ends the stanza. The song was published by the Playfords, in *The Plotting Papists' Litany,* in 1680. The tune is a ruder and therefore probably earlier version of the one given above.

## THE DUKE OF BERWICK'S MARCH,
## or WHY, SOLDIERS, WHY,
## or HOW STANDS THE GLASS AROUND.

*The Patron,* &c., Ballad Opera, 1729.

Why, soldiers, why
Should we be melancholy, boys?
Why, soldiers, why?
Whose business 'tis to die!
What! sighing? fie!
Damn fear, drink on, be jolly boys!
'Tis he, you, or I;
Cold, hot, wet, or dry,
We're always bound to follow, boys,
And scorn to fly.

'Tis but in vain,
(I mean not to upbraid you, boys),
'Tis but in vain
For soldiers to complain:
Should next campaign
Send us to Him who made us, boys,
We're free from pain;
But should we remain,
A bottle and kind landlady
Cures all again.

The song "Why, soldiers, why," is contained in a MS. book of poetry in the Advocates' Library, Edinburgh, under the title of the "Duke of Berwick's March." The tune is first found in *The Patron*, called *Why, soldiers, why;* and both words and music are to be found in *Vocal Music*, &c., 1775, vol. ii., p. 49, there called "A Soldier's Song." Shield introduced them into the *Siege of Gibraltar*.

## ON YONDER HIGH MOUNTAINS.

*The Cobblers' Opera*, 1729; *Silvia*, 1731.

I have not found any song or ballad commencing "On yonder high mountains," but "Over hills and high mountains" was a very popular ballad in the latter part of the preceding century, and the tune was often referred to.

This is evidently a ballad tune, and as the metre of "Over hills and high mountains" exactly suits it, as well as the character of the words, it is probably the right air.

THE LATER POPULAR MUSIC. 137

Copies of "Over hills and high mountains" are in the Bagford Collection, 643, m. 10, p. 165, and in the Pepys Collection, iii. 165. The ballad is entitled "The Wandering Maiden ; or, True Love at length united," &c. : "to an *excellent new tune.*" "Printed by J. Deacon, at the Angel in Guiltspur Street, without Newgate." It commences thus :—

> "Over hills and high mountains long time have I gone ;
> Ah ! and down by the fountains, by myself all alone ;
> Through bushes and briars, being void of all care,
> Through perils and dangers for the loss of my dear."

In the Roxburghe Collection, ii. 470, is "True love without deceit," &c. : "to the tune of *Over hills and high mountains*" ; commencing :—

> "Unfortunate Strephon ! well may'st thou complain,
> Since thy cruel Phillis thy love doth disdain."

Also ii. 508, "The Wandering Virgin ; or, The Coy Lass well fitted : or, The Answer to the Wandering Maiden," &c. : "to a pleasant new tune, *Over hills and high mountains.*"

Both the above were printed by P. Brooksby.


## ON THE COLD GROUND, OR I PRETHEE, LOVE, TURN TO ME.

*The Dancing Master,* 1665 ; *Musick's Delight on the Cithren,* 1666 ; *Apollo's Banquet for the Treble Violin,* 1669.

I'll crown thee with a garland of straw, then
And I'll marry thee with a rush ring ;
My frozen hopes shall thaw, then,
And merrily we will sing :
O turn to me, my dear love,
And prithee, love, turn to me,
For thou art the man that alone canst,
Procure my liberty.

But if thou wilt harden thy heart still,
And be deaf to my pitiful moan,
Then I must endure the smart still,
And tumble in straw alone ;
Yet still I cry, O turn love,
And prithee, love, turn to me,
For thou art the man that alone art
The cause of my misery.

This is a song sung by "a mad shepherdess" in the play of *The Rivals*, an alteration of Fletcher's *Two Noble Kinsmen*, written by Sir William Davenant, and first performed in or about the year 1664. The tune was ascribed to Matthew Lock.

The words were reprinted in *Merry Drollery Complete*, Part II., 1670, under the title of "Phillis, her Lamentation"; and in the same, a parody on it, called "Women's Delight." Another parody, "My Lodging is on the Cold Boards," is in Howard's play, *All Mistaken*, 1672. Then the original in *The New Academy of Compliments*, 1694, 1713, &c.; in *Vocal Music, or The Songster's Companion*, 8vo, 1775; in Johnson's *Lottery Song Book*, N.D.; and fifty others. It was lengthened into a ballad, and became equally popular in that form. A copy is in the Roxburghe Collection, ii. 423, "printed by and for W. O[nley] for A. M[ilbourne], and sold by C. Bates, at the Sun and Bible in Pye Corner."

The following ballads, sung to the tune, are in the Roxburghe Collection:—

Vol. ii. 88. "The Courteous Health; or, The Merry Boys of the Times.

> "'He that loves sack, doth nothing lack,
> If he but loyal be;
> He that denies Bacchus' supplies
> Shews mere hypocrisy.'

"To a new tune, *Come, boys, fill us a bumper; or, My Lodging is on the Cold Ground;*" with the burden, "A Brimmer to the King," and beginning:—

> "Come, boys, fill us a bumper
> We'll make the nation roar;
> She's grown sick of a Rumper,
> That sticks on the old score," &c.

Vol. iii. 196. "The Old Man's Complaint; or, The Unequal-matcht Couple," &c.: "tune of *I prithee, love, turn to me.*"

Vol. ii. 520. "Wit bought at a dear rate," &c.: "to the tune of *Turn, love, I prethee, love, turn to me.*" Printed by F. Coles, and begins:—

> "If all the world my mind did know,
> I would not care a pin," &c.

Vol. iii. 144. "The Faithful Lover's Farewell; or, Private News from Chatham," &c.: "to the tune of *My Lodging is on the Cold Ground.*" "Printed for Sarah Tyus, at the Three Bibles, on London Bridge." Begins:—

> "As I in a meadow was walking,
> Some two or three weeks ago,
> I heard two lovers a-talking,
> And trampling to and fro," &c.

There are many more in other collections of ballads; as, for instance, in that formed by Mr. Halliwell (see Nos. 106, 118, 161, and 335, in the printed catalogue); but enough have already been quoted to prove the extreme and long-continued popularity of *My Lodging is on the Cold Ground*.

The only difficulty is in ascertaining the precise time when Matthew Lock's tune was discarded, and that now universally known took its place. I have not found the former in print after 1670, but it may have been included in some of the editions of *Apollo's Banquet*, between 1670 and 1690, which I have never seen. The air now known is printed on all the broadsides, with music, of the last century; and it is possible that the ballad-singers may have altogether discarded Matthew Lock's tune, and adopted another,—a liberty subsequently taken with Carey's air to his ballad of *Sally in our Alley*, although the original was quite as melodious as the one substituted. There is a song to the tune of *My Lodging, it is on the Cold Ground* in *The Rape of Helen*, 1737, but that ballad-opera is printed without music.

The following is the popular air, with the words usually sung:—

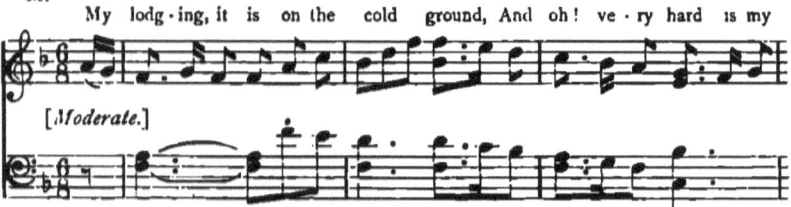

My lodg-ing, it is on the cold ground, And oh! ve-ry hard is my
[*Moderate.*]

fare, But that which grieves me more, love, Is the cold-ness of my dear.

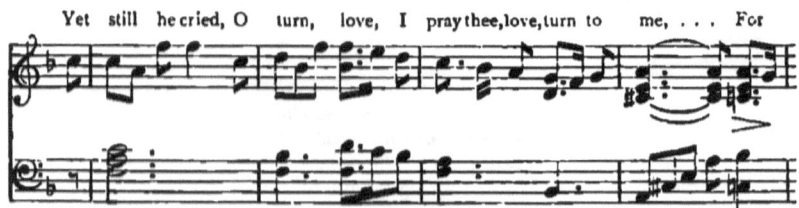

Yet still he cried, O turn, love, I pray thee, love, turn to me, . . . For

thou art the on-ly girl, love, That art a-dor'd by me.

With a garland of straw I'll crown thee, love,
I'll marry thee with a rush ring;
Thy frozen heart shall melt with love,
So, merrily I shall sing.
    Yet still he cried, &c.

But, if thou wilt harden thy heart, love,
And be deaf to my pitiful moan,
Then I must endure the smart, love,
And tumble in straw all alone.
    Yet still he cried &c.

The words and music are printed in *Vocal Music, or The Songster's Companion*, 8vo, 1775, and it has been a stock-song in print from that time.

## THE LEATHER BOTTLE.

*Pills to purge Melancholy*, 1707, vol. i.

'Twas God a-bove that made all things, The heav'ns the earth and all there-in:

The ships that on the sea do swim, To guard from foes that none come in.

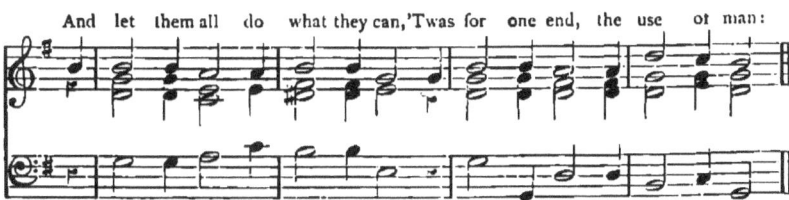

And let them all do what they can, 'Twas for one end, the use of man:

So I wish in heav'n his soul may dwell, That first found out the leather bot-tel.

Now, what do you say to these cans of wood?
Oh no, in faith they cannot be good;
For if the bearer fell by the way,
Why, on the ground your liquor doth lay:
But had it been in a leather bottel,
Although he had fallen, all had been well.
    So I wish in heav'n, &c.

Then what do you say to these glasses fine?
Oh, they shall have no praise of mine,
For if you chance to touch the brim,
Down falls the liquor and all therein;[1]
But had it been in a leather bottel,
And the stopple in, all had been well.
    So I wish, &c.

\* \* \* \* \*

[2] There's never a Lord, an Earl, or Knight,
But in this bottle doth take delight;
For when he's hunting of the deer,
He oft doth wish for a bottle of beer.
Likewise the man that works in the wood,
A bottle of beer will oft do him good.
    So I wish, &c.

And when the bottle at last grows old,
And will good liquor no longer hold,
Out of the side you may make a clout,
To mend your shoes when they're worn out;
Or take and hang it up on a pin,
'Twill serve to put hinges and odd things in.
    So I wish, &c.

---

[[1] In a broadside of this ballad in Anthony Wood's collection, in the Bodleian Library, there are two more lines at this place:—
    "It may be for a small abuse,
    a young man may his service lose."
The tune ordered in this broadside is *The Bottel-maker's Delight*. Whether this is the one given above I have no means of knowing. In the case of one or more superfluous couplets, one or more sections of the tune could very well be repeated. From the nature of the tune repetition would cause no inconvenience.—ED.]

[[2] This stanza strongly suggests an origin older than the seventeenth century.—ED.]

Although I have not found any copy of this ballad printed before the reign of Charles II., there appears reason for believing it to be of much earlier date. The irregularity in the number of lines in each stanza—eight, ten, and sometimes twelve in the earlier copies—gives it the character rather of a minstrel production, such as Richard Sheale's "Chevy Chace," than of anything by the Eldertons, Delonys, or Martin Parkers of the reigns of Elizabeth and James, who all observed a just number of lines in their ballads.

Another reason for thinking it old arises from the manner in which it begins. A very early ballad, written by a priest in the reign of Queen Mary (a copy of which is in the library of the Society of Antiquaries), has a very similar opening, and the metre is so like that it might be sung to the same tune. It is entitled "A new Ballade of the Marigolde," and begins thus :—

> "The God above, for man's delight,
> Hath heere ordaynde every thing,
> Sonne, Moone and Sterres shinying so bright,
> With all kind fruites, that here doth spring,
> And flowres that are so flourishyng:
> Amonges all which that I beholde
> (As to my minde best contentyng),
> I doo commende the Marigolde."

In the seventh stanza :—

> "To Marie our Queene, that flowre so sweete,
> This Marigolde I doo apply,
> For that the name doth serve so meete
> And properle in each partie,
> For her enduring paciently
> The stormes of such as list to scolde
> At her dooynges, without cause why,
> Loth to see spring this Marigolde."

At the end, " God save the Queene. Quod William Forrest, *Preest*."[1] Printed by Richard Lant, in Aldersgate Street.

Copies of *The Leather Bottle* are to be found in the Bagford, Roxburghe, and other Collections; in the list of those printed by Thackeray; in *Wit and Drollery*, 1682; in *The New Academy of Compliments*, 1694 and 1713; in *Pills to purge Melancholy;* in Dryden's *Miscellany Poems;* and in a succession of others to the present day. Mr. Sandys contributed a Somersetshire version to Mr. Dixon's *Ballads and Songs of the Peasantry of England.*

---

[1] This is probably the William Forrest of Christ Church, Oxford, who was chaplain to Queen Mary at the time of her accession to the throne.
[Probably also the same William Forrest who made a valuable collection of early sixteenth-century church music (chiefly masses), which was afterwards presented by Dr. Heyther to the Music School in Oxford.—ED.]

## SWEET WILLIAM'S FAREWELL TO BLACK-EY'D SUSAN.

*Watts' Musical Miscellany*, vol. iv. 1730; Half-sheets and Broadsides with music, 1730 and later; The Ballad-Operas.

The words of "Sweet William's Farewell" are by Gay, and are included among his published poems. The music is by Richard Leveridge.

[Leveridge published, in 1727, a collection of his songs which does not include "Sweet William's Farewell." The above version (with bass), which is the earliest I can find with a date, is from the fourth volume of Watts' *Musical Miscellany*, issued in 1730. The song may therefore have been composed in the interval.

Leveridge, according to all accounts, was a genial and popular personage, possessed of a fine voice and a method at that time acceptable, and possibly the success of his songs was in some measure due to these advantages. He was a poor composer, and this early version of his famous song will probably be considered much inferior to the one now generally received. But there have been better versions than either; and I here give below one dating from about the close of the century, when the alterations gradually made by performers had brought the tune to what appears to be its best condition. As the song would seem to be intended for a bass or baritone voice, I have for once placed the tune in the lower half of the harmony, and as it is not readily distinguishable in that situation I have also given it separately.—ED.]

William, who high upon the yard
  Rock'd with the billows to and fro,
Soon as her well-known voice he heard
  He sighed, and cast his eyes below:
The cord slides swiftly through his glowing hands,
And quick as lightning on the deck he stands.

     \*     \*     \*     \*     \*

O Susan, Susan, lovely dear,
  My vows shall ever true remain,
Let me kiss off that falling tear;
  We only part to meet again.
Change as ye list, ye winds; my heart shall be
The faithful compass that still points to thee.

Believe not what the landsmen say
  Who tempt with doubts thy constant mind;
They'll tell thee sailors, when away,
  In every port a mistress find:
Yes, yes, believe them when they tell thee so,
For thou art present wheresoe'er I go.

  \*     \*     \*     \*     \*

The boatswain gave the dreadful word,
  The sails their swelling bosoms spread;
No longer must she stay aboard;
  They kissed, she sigh'd, he hung his head.
Her lessening boat unwilling rows to land;
"Adieu!" she cries; and wav'd her lily hand.

## COME, OPEN THE DOOR, SWEET BETTY.

Ballad Operas; *Flora*, 1729; *Cobblers' Opera*, 1729; *Achilles*, 1733; *The Livery Rake*, there called "O fly from this place."

In the Pepys Collection, iii. 62, and in the Roxburghe, ii. 238, are copies of this ballad, entitled "John's Earnest Request; or, Betty's compassionate love extended to him in a time of distress: to *a pleasant new tune* much in request." Printed for P. Brooksby, at the Golden Ball in Pye Corner. It consists of nine stanzas, the first of which begins :—

"Come, open the door, sweet Betty,[1]
For 'tis a cold winter's night ;
It rains and it blows and it thunders,
And the moon it does give no light," &c.

"Come, open the door, sweet Betty," appears in the first part of a tune called *Tom Nokes' Jigg*.[2] The time is different; it is quick, and in 9/8 measure; but evidently one is founded upon the other, or perhaps both are from the same root. It is to be found in the first edition of *Apollo's Banquet*, 1669, and is as follows:—

[1] In Burns' remarks on the songs in Johnson's *Scot's Musical Museum*, he speaks of "old words" to "Blink o'er the burn, sweet Betty," and says, "All that I remember are:—

'Blink over the burn, sweet Betty,
It is a cauld winter night ;
It rains, it hails, it thunders,
The moon she gives nae light,'" &c.

The Scotch tune, "Blink over the burn, sweet Betty," bears no resemblance to "Come, open the door, sweet Betty," nor do the Scotch words, in an early collection, resemble the English ; but the song quoted by Burns, and since adopted in Wood's *Songs of Scotland*, is evidently taken from the English ballad.

[2] Nokes was a favourite actor with the public in the reign of Charles II.

## CUPID'S TREPAN.

*Flora*, 1729; *The Devil to pay*, and many other Ballad Operas.

This was a very popular ballad tune, and it acquired a variety of names from the different ballads that were sung to it at different periods. I have not, however, observed any of these to have been issued by printers earlier than those of the reign of Charles II. (Thackeray, Coles, &c.); but there are many extant of later date.

Among the various names of the tune may be cited, *Cupid's Trappan; Up the green forest; Bonny, bonny bird; Brave Boys; The Twitcher; A damsel I'm told;* and *I have left the world as the world found me.*

The following ballads were sung to it:—

"Cupid's Trappan, or The Scorner scorned, or The Willow turned into Carnation: described in The Ranting Resolution of a Forsaken Maid. To *a pleasant new tune now all in fashion.*" It commences:—

> "Once did I love a bonny brave bird,
>   And thought he had been all my own,
> But he lov'd another far better than me,
>   And has taken his flight and is flown, *Brave Boys*,
>   *And has taken his flight and is flown.*
>
> "Up the green forest, and down the green forest,
>   Like one much distressed in mind,
> I hoopt and I hoopt, and I flung up my hood,
>   But my bonnie bird I could not find, *Brave Boys*.
>   *But my bonny bird I could not find.*"

There are many copies of this ballad, and among them two will be found in the Douce and Ewing Collections; one of which is entitled "Cupid's Trappan; or, Up the green forest," &c.

Other ballads to the tune, under one or other of the names given above, will be found in the Roxburghe Collection, ii. 260, 262, and 347, and iii. 109; also in the *Musical Companion*, 1741, and *St. Cecilia; or, The British Songster*, 1782.

## THE DOUBTING VIRGIN, OR WOMAN'S WORK IS NEVER DONE.

*Momus turned Fabulist* (Ballad Opera), 1729, &c.

This tune has a variety of names, derived from different ballads that were sung to it. Among these are *The Doubting Virgin; or, Shall I, shall I; O that I had never married; Woman's work is never done; The Soldier's Departure*, &c.

In the Douce Collection, p. 190, and Roxburghe, vol. ii., p. 421, is "Shall I, shall I, no, no, no," &c. Tune of *The Doubting Virgin*, commencing :—

"Pretty Betty, now come to me,
Thou hast set my heart on fire,"

and having the burden :—

"Never dally, shall I? shall I?
Still she answered, No, no, no."

Whenever the tune of *The Doubting Virgin* is referred to in the Douce Collection, either Mr. Douce or some prior possessor has pencilled against it, "O that I had never married" as the other name.

"O that I had never married" is the first line of "Woman's work is never done, or The Crown Garland of Princely Pastime and Mirth ; the Woman has the worst of it, or her work is never done. To the tune of *The Doubting Virgin*." A copy of this is in Mr. Payne Collier's Collection ; it consists of seven stanzas, and begins :—

"O that I had never married,
Since I lead a careful life ;
Things with me are strangely carried
Now I am become a wife.
Whilst that he doth take his pleasure
(Lest he should to ruin run),
Here I labour out of measure,
*Woman's work is never done.*"

Others to the tune of *The Doubting Virgin* are "Real Reality ; or, The Soldier's Loyalty," &c., Pepys, iv. 43 ; "The Bleeding Lover," &c., Roxburghe, ii. 33 ; and others again in the same volume, at pp. 111, 180, 206, and 494.

## THE LATER POPULAR MUSIC.

In the Bagford Collection, 643, m. 10, p. 99, is "The Soldier's Departure, to a pleasant new tune," or *The Doubting Virgin;* and at p. 98, one to the tune of *The Soldier's Departure.*

In Dr. John Leyden's MS. of *Lyra-Viol Music,* formerly in the possession of Mr. G. F. Graham, of Edinburgh, is another tune called *Women's work will never be done,* which is as follows:—

To this tune probably was sung another ballad in the Roxburghe Collection, i. 534, also called "Woman's work is never done," but in a different metre from the one quoted above:—

"As I was wand'ring on the way,
I heard a married woman say,
That she had lived a sorry life
Ever since the time she was made a wife.

"For why, quoth she, my labour's hard,
And all my pleasures are debarred;
Both morning, evening, night, and noon,
I'm sure a woman's work is never done, &c.

"To a delicate Northern tune, *A Woman's work is never done; or, The Bed's-making.*"

## THE OXFORDSHIRE TRAGEDY.

*The Cobblers' Opera,* 1729; *The Village Opera,* 1729.

>Down by a crystal river side,
>A gallant bower I espied,
>Where a fair lady made great moan,
>With many a bitter sigh and groan.
>
>Alas! quoth she, my love's unkind,
>My sighs and tears he will not mind;
>But he is cruel unto me,
>Which causes all my misery, &c.

The ballad is in the Pepys Collection, v. 285. "The Constant Lady and False-hearted Squire: being a relation of a Knight's Daughter, near Woodstock in Oxfordshire, that dy'd for love of a Squire: *to a new tune.*" London, printed for R. B., near Fleet Street.

The ballad is in four parts, the third and fourth of which, being in a different metre, must have been sung to another air.

"As I walk'd forth to take the air," is the second line of the first part, and the tune is often referred to under that title.

In the Douce Collection, 44, is a black-letter ballad of "Cupid's Conquest; or, Will the Shepherd and fair Kate of the Green, both united together in pure love: to a tune, *As I went forth to take the air;*" commencing:—

>"Now am I tost on waves of love;
>Here like a ship that's under sail," &c.

and in the Roxburghe, ii. 149, "The Faithful Lovers of the West: tune, *As I walkt forth to take the air.*"

In Mr. Payne Collier's Collection is "The Unfortunate Sailor's Garland, with an account how his parents murdered him for love of his gold." It is in two parts, and both to the tune of *The Oxfordshire Tragedy*. After four lines of exordium, it begins thus:—

> "Near Bristol liv'd a man of fame,
> But I'll forbear to tell his name;
> He had one son and daughter bright,
> In whom he took a great delight," &c.;

Another Garland, called "The Cruel Parents; or, The Two Faithful Lovers," is to the tune of *The Oxfordshire Lady*, and in the same metre.

## TO ALL YOU LADIES NOW AT LAND.

Watts' *Musical Miscellany*, vol. iii. 1730; *Convivial Songster*, 1782; in the Ballad Operas of *The Jovial Crew, The Cobblers' Opera, The Lover's Opera, The Court Legacy, Polly, A Cure for a Scold*, &c.; and in *Pills to purge Melancholy*, vi. 272.

For though the Muses should prove kind,
And fill our empty brain ;
Yet if rough Neptune rouse the wind
To wave the azure main,
Our paper, pen, and ink, and we,
Roll up and down our ships at sea.
With a fa la, &c.

Then if we write not by each post,
Think not we are unkind ;
Nor yet conclude our ships are lost
By Dutchmen or by wind :
Our tears we'll send a speedier way,
The tide shall bring them twice a-day.
With a fa la, &c.

The king, with wonder and surprise,
Will swear the seas grow bold ;
Because the tides will higher rise,
Than e'er they did of old :
But let him know it is our tears
Bring floods of grief to Whitehall stairs.
With a fa la, &c.

Should foggy Opdam chance to know
Our sad and dismal story ;
The Dutch would scorn so weak a foe,
And quit their fort at Goree :
For what resistance can they find
From men who've left their hearts behind ?
With a fa la, &c.

Let wind and weather do its worst,
Be you to us but kind ;
Let Dutchmen vapour, Spaniards curse,
No sorrow shall we find :
'Tis then no matter how things go,
Or who's our friend, or who's our foe.
With a fa la, &c.

To pass our tedious hours away,
We throw a merry main ;
Or else at serious ombre play ;
But why should we in vain
Each other's ruin thus pursue ?
We were undone when we left you.
With a fa la, &c.

But now our fears tempestuous grow,
And cast our hopes away :
Whilst you regardless of our woe,
Sit careless at a play :
Perhaps permit some happier man
To kiss your hand, or flirt your fan.
With a fa la, &c.

When any mournful tune you hear,
That dies in every note ;
As if it sigh'd with each man's care,
For being so remote :
Think then how often love we've made
To you, when all those tunes were play'd.
With a fa la, &c.

In justice you cannot refuse,
To think of our distress ;
When we for hopes of honour lose
Our certain happiness :
All those designs are but to prove
Ourselves more worthy of your love.
With a fa la, &c.

And now we've told you all our loves,
And likewise all our fears ;
In hopes this declaration moves
Some pity for our tears :
Let's hear of no inconstancy,
We have too much of that at sea.
With a fa la, &c.

This ballad was written by Lord Buckhurst, afterwards Earl of Dorset, when at sea during the first Dutch war, 1664-5. It has been said to have been written " the night before the engagement " ; but, in all probability, was penned during the Duke of York's first cruise, in November, 1664, when an action was avoided by the Dutch retiring to port.

The proof is, that it is mentioned by Pepys in his Diary, under the date of Jan. 2nd, 1664-5. He says, "To my Lord Brouncker's by appointment, in the Piazza, Covent Garden ; where I occasioned much mirth with a ballet I brought with me, made from the seamen at sea to the ladies in town."

The statement that it was "made the night before the engagement," which took place in June, 1665, is irreconcilable with Pepys' possession of a copy in the preceding January, and has been carefully analysed by Lord Braybrooke, in his notes upon Pepys' Diary, v. 241, edit. 1849. It rests upon the authority of Matthew Prior, who was born in 1664, and who had probably heard the story with a little embellishment.

In *Merry Drollery Complete*, 1670, is the song "My mistress is a shuttlecock," to this tune. In *A Pill to purge State Melancholy*, 12mo, 1715, is "The Soldiers' Lamentation for the loss of their General," &c. : to the tune of *To you fair ladies ;* and the same was printed in broadside with the date of 1712. Also, "News from Court, a ballad to the tune of *To all you ladies now at land*, by Mr. Pope," 1719. In the *Gentleman's Magazine* for July, 1731, "To all you ladies now at Bath."

## SIR GUY.

*Robin Hood* (Ballad Opera), 1730.

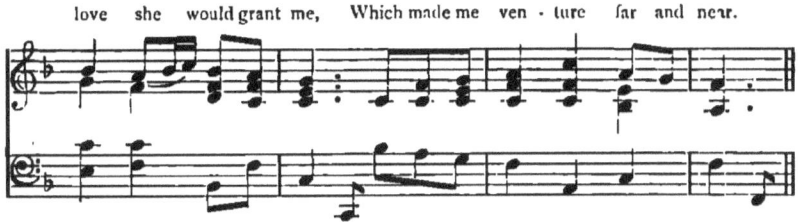

This ballad was entered to Richard Jones on Jan. 5th, 1591-2, as "A plesante songe of the valiant actes of Guy of Warwicke: to the tune of *Was ever man so tost in love.*" The copy in the Bagford Collection, p. 19, is entitled "A pleasant song of the valiant deeds of chivalry achieved by that noble knight, Sir Guy of Warwick, who, for the love of fair Phillis, became a hermit, and died in a cave of a craggy rock a mile distant from Warwick. Tune, *Was ever man, &c.*" Other copies are in the Pepys Collection; Roxburghe, iii. 50; and in Percy's *Reliques*, series 3, book ii.

It is quoted in Fletcher's *Knight of the Burning Pestle*, act ii., sc. 8; and in *The Little French Lawyer*, act ii., sc. 3.

William of Nassyngton (about 1480) mentions stories of Sir Guy as usually sung by minstrels at feasts. Puttenham, in his *Art of Poetry*, 1589, says they were then commonly sung to the harp at Christmas dinners and bride-ales for the recreation of the lower classes. And in Dr. King's *Dialogues of the Dead*: "It is the negligence of our ballad singers that makes us to be talked of less than others: for who, almost, besides *St. George, King Arthur, Bevis, Guy*, and *Hickathrift*, are in the chronicles."—(Vol. i., p. 153.)

## THERE WAS AN OLD FELLOW AT WALTHAM CROSS,
## OR TAUNTON DEAN.

*The Jovial Crew* (Ballad Opera), 1731.

This is quoted as an old song in Brome's play, *The Jovial Crew*, which was acted at the Cock-pit, in Drury Lane, in 1641. It is also in the *Antidote against Melancholy*, 1661.

*The Jovial Crew* was turned into a ballad opera in 1731, and this song retained. The tune was then printed under the name of *Taunton Dean*.

## THE BAILIFF'S DAUGHTER.

*The Jovial Crew* (Ballad Opera), 1731.

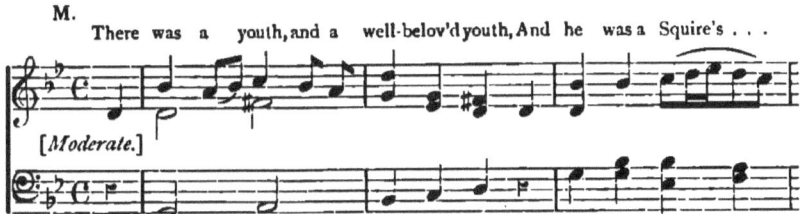

Yet she was coy, and would not believe
That he did love her so,
No, nor at any time would she
Any countenance to him show, &c.

Dr. Rimbault found this tune in a lute MS., formerly in the possession of the Rev. Mr. Gostling, of Canterbury, under the name of *The Jolly Pinder*. In the ballad opera of *The Jovial Crew*, 1731, the same air is called *The Baily's Daughter of Islington*.

The better known tune is traditional merely.

Copies of this ballad are in the Roxburghe, Pepys, and Douce Collections; it is printed by Ritson among the ancient ballads in his *English Songs*, and by Percy (*Reliques*, series 3, book ii., No. 8).

In the Roxburghe, ii. 457, and Douce, 230, it is entitled "True Love Requited; or, The Bailiff's Daughter of Islington: to a *North-country* tune, or *I have a good old mother at home.*" In other copies it is to "I have a good *old woman* at home," and "I have a good *wife* at home."

In the Douce, 32, is a ballad called "Crums of Comfort for the Youngest Sister, &c.: to a pleasant new *West-country* tune;" beginning "I have a good *old father* at home."

## THERE LIVES A LASS UPON THE GREEN.

*The Jovial Crew,* 1731.

But where they danc'd their cheerful round,
    The morning would disclose,
For where their nimble feet do bound
    Each flow'r unbidden grows:
The daisy, fair as maids in May,
The cowslip in his gold array,
    And blushing violet, 'rose.

The original song has not been found. The words here given are those of the song in *The Jovial Crew*, where it is thus prefaced by Rachel, who sings it:—" I remember an old song of my nurse's, every word of which she believ'd as much as her Psalter, that used to make me long, when I was a girl, to be abroad in a moonlight night."

## THREE MERRY MEN OF KENT.

*The Jovial Crew,* 1731.

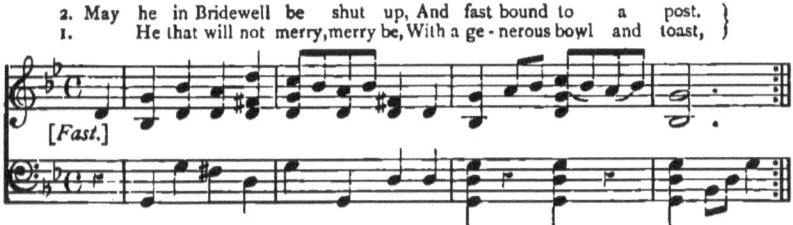

He that will not merry, merry be,
　And take his glass in course,
May he be obliged to drink small beer,
　Ne'er a penny in his purse.
　　*Let him be merry, merry there, &c.*

He that will not merry, merry be,
　With a company of jolly boys,
May he be plagued with a scolding wife,
　To confound him with her noise.
　　*Let him be merry, merry there, &c.*

The name at the head is that given to the tune in *The Jovial Crew*, but the song of "Three Merry Men of Kent" has not been discovered. The words given in the ballad opera form the fourth stanza of a song which is sometimes to be met with in eighteenth-century broadsides and collections. That stanza is not suitable to this work, but the three which precede it have been here printed with the tune.

## LOVELY NANCY.

*The Jovial Crew.*

# THE LATER POPULAR MUSIC. 163

You see the sad fate we poor maidens endure;
Cannot charity move you to grant us a cure?
How hard is your heart, how unkind is your eye,
If nothing can move you, good Sir, to comply.

This is one of the airs contained in the folio edition of *The Jovial Crew* (which has the basses to the airs), but not in the octavo. It was added after the first performance. The above words were sung by the female beggars in the opera.

Four lines of the original words to the tune are in Walsh's *Select Aires for the Guitar, &c* :—

"How can you, lovely Nancy, thus cruelly slight
A swain who is wretched when banish'd your sight?
Who for your sake alone thinks life worth his care,
But which soon, if you frown on, must end in despair."

## OLD HEWSON THE COBBLER.

*The Jovial Crew* and *The Grub Street Opera* (Ballad Operas), 1731.

The words of the song have not been recovered; but there can be little doubt that they were a political satire upon Colonel Hewson, who was one of Charles I.'s judges, and of those who signed his death-warrant.

John Hewson was originally a cobbler, and had but one eye. He took up arms on the side of the Parliament, and being a man of courage and resolution, soon rose to be a colonel in their army. He was knighted by Cromwell, and afterwards made one of his Lords. He quitted England immediately before the Restoration, and died at Amsterdam in 1662.

There are numerous allusions to his former trade, and to his one eye, in the Cavalier songs. For instance, in "A Quarrel betwixt Tower Hill and Tyburne" (to be found in *Merry Drollery Complete; Loyal Songs*, &c.):—

> "There is single-eyed Hewson, the Cobbler of Fate,
> Translated into buff and feather;
> But *bootless* are all his *seams* of state,
> When the *soul* is ript from the upper leather."

Two complete songs about him are in the Bagford Collection (643, m. 9, Brit. Mus.); and in *Loyal Songs*, vol. ii.

The first, "A Hymn to the Gentle Craft; or, Hewson's Lamentation: to the tune of *The Blind Beggar*." But the name of this tune was selected only as a sneer at his one eye; the words are not in a metre that could be sung to it:—

> "Listen awhile to what I shall say
> Of a blind cobbler that's gone astray,
> Out of the Parliament's highway:
> Good people, pity the blind," &c.

The second is "The Cobbler's Last Will and Testament; or, The Lord Hewson's Translation:—

> "To Christians all I greeting send,
> That they may learn their *souls* to mend,
> By viewing of my cobbler's *end*," &c.

## THE SAILOR'S COMPLAINT.

*Walsh's Musical Miscellany*, vol. iv.

Come, and listen to my ditty,
    All ye jolly hearts of gold ;
Lend a brother Tar your pity,
    Who was once so stout and bold.
But the arrows of Cupid,
    Alas ! have made me rue ;
Sure, true love was ne'er so treated,
    As am I by scornful Sue.

When I landed first at Dover,
    She appear'd a goddess bright ;
From foreign parts I'd just come over,
    And was struck with so fair a sight.
On shore pretty Sukey walked,
    Near to where our frigate lay,
And altho' so near the landing,
    I, alas ! was cast away.

When first I hail'd my pretty creature,
    The delight of land and sea ;
No man ever saw a sweeter,
    I'd have kept her company ;
I'd have fain made her my true love,
    For better, or for worse ;
But alas ! I cou'd not compass her,
    For to steer the marriage course.

\*   \*   \*   \*

Long I wonder'd why my jewel
    Had the heart to use me so,
Till I found, by often sounding,
    She'd another love in tow :
So farewell, hard-hearted Sukey,
    I'll my fortune seek at sea,
And try in a more friendly latitude,
    Since in yours I cannot be.

In the ballad-opera of *Silvia; or, The Country Burial*, printed in 1731, the song, "On some rock, by seas surrounded," is adapted to the tune, and the old name is there given as "How happy are young lovers"; so, also, in *Robin Hood*, 1730.

The title, "How happy are young lovers," is the first line of the ballad of "The Distracted Sailor," a copy of which is in the Douce Collection, and a second in that of Mr. J. M. Gutch. In the latter copy it is said to be to the tune of *What is greater joy or pleasure*, which carries the air a stage further back.

Many other sea songs were sung to this air. Among them, Glover's ballad of "Hosier's Ghost" (commencing, "As near Portobello lying"), and "Admiral Vernon's Answer to Admiral Hosier's Ghost" ("Hosier! with indignant sorrow"). These are reprinted in Halliwell's *Early Naval Ballads of England*.

But the most famous is "Cease, Rude Boreas," written, according to Ritson and others, by G. A. Stevens.


## THE DUSTY MILLER.

Walsh's *Compleat Country Dancing Master*; Wright's *Country Dances*, i. 24; Thompson's *Country Dances*, ii. 93, &c.

## CHESHIRE ROUNDS.

*The Dancing Master*, ed. 11, &c. ; Walsh's *Compleat Country Dancing Master*, vol. i. ; *Polly*, and other ballad operas.

Mr. George Daniel, in his *Merry England*, remarks that the only known portrait of Dogget, the actor (of coat and badge notoriety), is a small engraving representing him dancing the *Cheshire Round*. Mr. Daniel prints one of Dogget's play-bills, issued in 1691, and the following from other bills of the time of William III., showing how popular the dance then was :—" In Bartholomew Fair, at the Coach-house on the pav'd stones at Hosier-Lane end, you will see a Black that dances the *Cheshire Rounds* to the admiration of all spectators."—" John Sleepe now keeps the Whelp and Bacon in Smithfield Rounds, where are to be seen a young lad that dances a *Cheshire Round* to the admiration of all people." A third and similar advertisement was issued by Michael Root.

*Cheshire Rounds* is one of the tunes called for by "the hobnailed fellows" in *A Second Tale of a Tub*, 8vo, 1715.

## SHROPSHIRE ROUNDS.

From the second volume of *The Dancing Master*, and the second volume of Walsh's *Compleat Country Dancing Master*.

## THERE WAS A PRETTY LASS AND A TENANT OF MY OWN.

The Broadsides, and many Ballad Operas.

Among the songs which were written to this tune, and attained popularity, are, "Sure marriage is a fine thing," from *The Beggars' Wedding* (reprinted in vol. v. of Watts's *Musical Miscellany*, 1731), and—

"I'm a bold recruiting sargeant,
From London I am come."

## DEATH AND THE LADY.

H. Carey's *Musical Century*, 1738 ; *Cobbler's Opera ; The Fashionable Lady*, and other Ballad Operas.

LADY.
What bold attempt is this? pray let me know
From whence you come, and whither I must go !
Shall I, who am a lady, stoop or bow
To such a pale-fac'd visage?   Who art thou?

### DEATH.

Do you not know me? Well, I'll tell you, then:
'Tis I who conquer all the sons of men!
No pitch of honour from my dart is free;
My name is Death! have you not heard of me?

### LADY.

Yes, I have heard of thee time after time;
But, being in the glory of my prime,
I did not think you would have called so soon.
Why must my sun go down before its noon? &c.

The ballad of "Death and the Lady" is printed in a small volume entitled *A Guide to Heaven*, 12mo, 1736; and it is twice mentioned in Goldsmith's popular tale, *The Vicar of Wakefield*, first printed in 1776.

The tune seems to be a very much corrupted version of the first part of *Fortune my Foe*.

The oldest copies of *Aim not too high* direct it to be sung to the tune of *Fortune*, but there is one class of ballads, said to be to the tune of *Aim not too high*, that could not well be sung to that air. The accent of *Fortune my Foe* is on the first syllable of each line; exactly agreeing with the tune. But these ballads on Death have the accent on the second, and agree with the tune of *Death and the Lady*. I suppose, then, that ballads to the tune of *Aim not too high* may be either to *Fortune*, or *Death and the Lady*; a point to be determined generally by the accent of the words.

## OLD KING COLE.

*Achilles* (Ballad Opera), 1733.

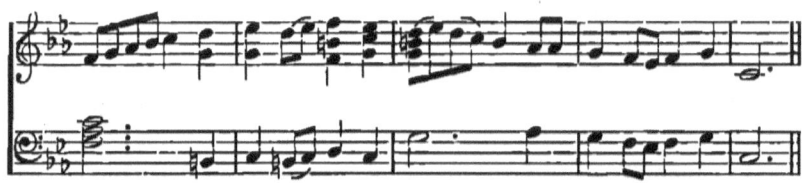

In *The Pleasant Historie of Thomas of Reading, or, The Sixe Worthie Yeomen of the West* (by Deloney).—London: Printed by Eliz. Allde for Robert Bird, 1632, is the legend of one Cole, a cloth maker, from which may perhaps descend the later allusions and songs; but if so, the intermediate links are lost.

Certainly, there was some joke or conventional meaning among Elizabethan dramatists, when they gave a man the name of Old Cole, which it is now difficult to discover. Gifford supposes it to be a nickname given to Ben Jonson by Dekker, because in the *Satiromastix*, where Horace says, "I'll lay my hands under your feet, Captain Tucca," Tucca answers, "Say'st thou to me so, old Cole? come, do it then"; but Dekker uses it elsewhere when there can be no allusion to Ben Jonson. Marston, too, in *The Malcontent*, makes Malevole apply it to a woman :—

> *Malevole to Maquarelle.* Ha, Dipsas! how dost thou, old Cole?
> *Maquarelle.* Old Cole!
> *Malevole.* Ay, old Cole; methinks thou liest like a brand under billets of green wood.

This play was printed in 1604, and dedicated to Ben Jonson, with whom Marston was then on the most friendly terms. It is true that Ben Jonson, in *Bartholomew Fair*, gives the name of Old Cole to the sculler in the puppet-show of Hero and Leander; but this was first acted in 1614, and Dekker's *Satiromastix* printed in 1602.

Dr. Wm. King, a humorous writer, who was born in 1663, quotes some of the words of "Old King Cole" in No. 6 of his *Useful Transactions;* but he mixes them up with those of " Four-and-twenty fiddlers all of a row."

> "Good King Cole,
> And he called for his bowl,
> And he called for his fiddlers three;
> And there was fiddle, fiddle,
> And twice fiddle, fiddle,
> For 'twas my lady's birthday;
> Therefore we keep holyday.
> And come to be merry."

## DOWN AMONG THE DEAD MEN.

The Broadsides; also in *The Dancing Master*, vol. iii., and Walsh's *Dancing Master*, vol. iii.

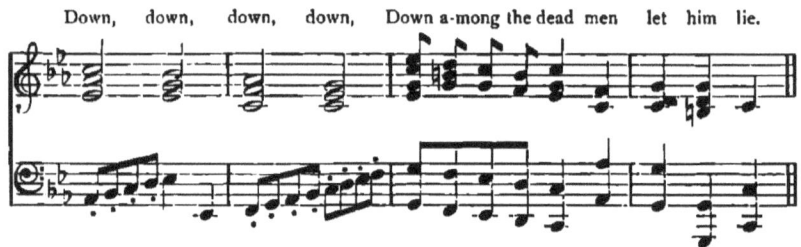

Let charming beauty's health go round,
In whom celestial joys are found,
And may confusion still pursue
The senseless woman-hating crew!
And they that woman's health deny,
Down among the dead men let them lie.

In smiling Bacchus' joys I'll roll,
Deny no pleasure to my soul;
Let Bacchus' health round briskly move,
For Bacchus is a friend to Love;
And he that will this health deny,
Down among the dead men let him die.

May love and wine their rites maintain,
And their united pleasures reign,
While Bacchus' treasure crowns the board,
We'll sing the joys that both afford;
And they that won't with us comply,
Down among the dead men let them lie.

The author of the words, whoever he may have been, had in mind the drinking-song in Fletcher's *Bloody Brother*, from which he borrowed two lines:—

"Best, while you have it, use your breath,
There is no drinking after death."

## A-HUNTING WE WILL GO.

*The Goldfinch*, Edinburgh, 1777, there ascribed to Dr. Arne; the Broadsides, &c.

        The wife around her husband throws
          Her arms, and begs his stay ;
        My dear, it rains, it hails and snows,
          You will not hunt to-day.
                But a-hunting we will go.

        A brushing fox in yonder wood,
          Secure to find we seek ;
        For why, I carried, sound and good,
          A cartload there last week.
                And a-hunting we will go.

        Away he goes, he flies the rout,
          Their steeds all spur and switch ;
        Some are thrown in, and some thrown out,
          And some thrown in the ditch.
                But a-hunting we will go.

        At length his strength to faintness worn,
          Poor Reynard ceases flight ;
        Then hungry, homeward, we return,
          To feast away the night.
                Then a-drinking we will go.

    This song was written by Henry Fielding, for his ballad opera of *Don Quixote in England* (1734): to the tune of *A-begging we will go;* but, on the broadsides with music—in *Vocal Music; or, The Songster's Companion*—in *The Vocal Enchantress*—in Dale's, and other collections, it is printed to this tune, and still sung to it.

    Several other songs have been written to the same air. Among them, "Father Paul"; commencing, "When grave divines preach up dull rules." A copy of this is in Dr. Burney's Collection, viii. 240, Brit. Mus. It has for burden or chorus :—

        "Here's a health to Father Paul,
          A health to Father Paul,
        For flowing bowls inspire the souls
          Of jolly friars all."

## HUMOURS OF THE BATH, OR THE SPRING'S A-COMING.

Watts's *Musical Miscellany*, 1729; *The Dancing Master*, vol. iii.; Walsh's *Dancing Master*, vol. iii.; *The Wedding*, and many other Ballad Operas.

"The Spring's a-coming" is the first line of a song called the "Bath Medley," by one Tony Aston.

## MOLLY'S HOOP.

Wright's *Country Dances*, vol. i.; the Broadsides, and several Ballad Operas.

M. What a fine thing have I seen to-day: O Mo-ther, a hoop!
[*Fast.*]

I must have one, you can-not say nay; O Mo-ther, a hoop!

For hus-bands are got-ten this way to be sure, Men's eyes and men's hearts they so

neat-ly al-lure; O Mo-ther, a hoop, a hoop! O Mo-ther, a hoop!

To this tune Cibber wrote the song "What Woman could do, I have tried, to be free," for his ballad opera of *Love in a Riddle*, 1729. It is also printed in *The Merry Musician*, ii. 7.

In *The Livery Rake*, 1733, the air takes the name of Cibber's song; but in *Damon and Phillida*, 1734, it is entitled "O Mother, a hoop!"

There are two versions of "O Mother, a hoop!" the one as a song, the other "A Dialogue between Miss Molly and her Mother about a hoop." A copy of the latter will be found in one of the collections in the British Museum (H. 1601, p. 532).

## O, GOOD ALE, THOU ART MY DARLING.

The Broadsides.

The brewer brew'd thee in his pan,
The tapster draws thee in his can;
Now I with thee will play my part,
And lodge thee next unto my heart.
    For 'tis O, good ale, &c.

Thou oft hast made my friends my foes,
And often made me pawn my clothes;
But since thou art so nigh my nose,
Come up, my friend,—and down he goes
    For 'tis O, good ale, &c.

The song is also in *The Banquet of Thalia*, York, 1790.

## COME, LET US DRINK ABOUT.

Half-sheet, with the music.

Wine cures the gout, the cholic, and the tisic,
And is for all men the very best of physic.

He that drinks small beer, and goes to bed sober,
Falls, as the leaves do, that die in October.

But he that drinks all day, and goes to bed mellow,
Lives as he ought to do, and dies a hearty fellow.

Another version will be found in *Vocal Miscellany*, vol. ii., 1734, and in *The Aviary*, 1745.

Both versions are founded on the following, from Fletcher's play, *The Bloody Brother; or, Rollo, Duke of Normandy*, act ii., sc. 2:—

" Drink to-day and drown all sorrow,
   You shall, perhaps, not do it to-morrow;
   Best, while you have it, use your breath,
   There is no drinking after death.

" Wine works the heart up, wakes the wit,
   There is no cure 'gainst age but it;
   It helps the head-ache, cough, and tisic,
   And is for all diseases physic.

" Then let us swill, boys, for our health;
   Who drinks well loves the commonwealth;
   And he that will to bed go sober,
   Falls with the leaf still in October."

## PRETTY POLLY OLIVER.

The Broadsides.

The broadside of this ballad was in print in quite recent times. It begins :—

"As pretty Polly Oliver lay musing in bed,
A comical fancy came into her head :
Nor father nor mother shall make me false prove,
I'll 'list for a soldier, and follow my love."

There is an old song on the Pretender, beginning :—

As Perkin one morning lay musing in bed,
The thought of three kingdoms ran much in his head ; "

which appears to be a parody of it.

## THE WOMEN ALL TELL ME.

Broadsides, with music, 1740-50.

The wo-men all tell me I'm false to my lass, That I quit my poor Chloe and stick to my glass; But to you men of rea-son, my

rea-sons I'll own, And if you don't like them, why let them a-lone.

   Although I have left her, the truth I'll declare ;
   I believe she was good, and I'm sure she was fair ;
   But goodness and charms in a bumper I see,
   That make it as good and as charming as she, &c.

The words are included in *The Wreath*, second edition, 1753 (and perhaps in the first edition, which I have not seen); also in *The Bullfinch, The Convivial Songster*, and many similar collections.

## THE BARKING BARBER.

This tune is to be found in two or three different forms, the variations having been caused by the different metres that have been adapted to it. For instance, one of the songs is "Date obolum Belisario," which has twelve syllables in the first line :—

"O Fortune ! how strangely are thy gifts awarded."

Another is the comic song of "Guy Fawkes," which, having sixteen syllables, requires fifteen notes in the first two bars of music :—

"I sing a doleful tragedy, Guy Fawkes that prince of sinisters."

The version printed above is the older of the two, sung to "O Fortune," &c.

## CARE, THOU CANKER OF OUR JOYS.

Care, thou can-ker of our joys, Now thy ty-rant reign is o'er;

[*Moderate.*]

Fill the merry, merry bowl, my boys, Join in bac-cha-na-lian roar.

Seize the villain, plunge him in;
See the hated miscreant dies: —
Mirth and all thy train come in,
Banish sorrow, tears, and sighs.

O'er our merry midnight bowls,
Oh! how happy shall we be;
Day was made for vulgar souls,
Night, my boys, for you and me.

This air is now better known as "When the rosy morn appearing," from the words which were sung to it, as a round, in the opera of *Rosina*. "Care, thou Canker of our joys," was written by the Rev. Dr. Grant, and I was informed by the late Ralph Banks, organist of Rochester Cathedral, that the tune was composed by John Garth, of Durham, the adapter of English words to Marcello's Psalms. It has never been published with any author's name.

## SMILING POLLY, OR THE KEEL ROW.

Thompson's 200 *Country Dances*, 1765.

O wha's like my Johnny,
Sae leish, sae blithe, sae bonny?
He's foremost among the mony
    Keel lads o' coaly Tyne :
He'll set and row so tightly,
Or in the dance—so sprightly—
He'll cut and shuffle sightly ;
    'Tis true—were he not mine.

He wears a blue bonnet,
Blue bonnet, blue bonnet ;
He wears a blue bonnet,—
    A dimple in his chin :
And weel may the keel row,
The keel row, the keel row ;
And weel may the keel row,
    That my laddie's in.

The earliest form in which I have observed this tune in print is as a country dance, entitled *Smiling Polly*. In several of the collections of the last century, such as that mentioned above at the head, it is so included. In these copies the second part of the tune differs.

The words of *The keel row* are in Ritson's *Northumberland Garland*, 1793; in Bell's *Rhymes of the Northern Bards*, 1812, and in several later collections.

### NANCY DAWSON, OR MISS DAWSON'S HORNPIPE.

*Love in a Village*, 1762; many collections of Country Dances.

Of all the girls in our town, The black, the fair, the

red, the brown, That dance and prance it up and down, There's

none like Nan - cy Daw - son. Her ea - sy mien, her shape so neat, She

foots, she trips, she looks so sweet, Her ev' - ry mo - tion's

See how she comes to give surprise,
With joy and pleasure in her eyes ;
To give delight she always tries,
So means my Nancy Dawson, &c.

The above words are to be found in *The Bullfinch*, and other collections, as well as under one of the engraved portraits of this celebrated dancer.[1]

The children's tune of *Here we go round the Mulberry Bush* is nothing but *Nancy Dawson*.

## BRIGHTON CAMP, OR THE GIRL I'VE LEFT BEHIND ME.

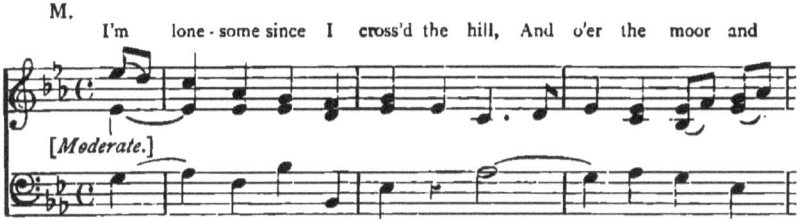

---

[1] One of her portraits is at the Garrick Club; and there are four different prints of her, one of which, by Spooner, is in Dr. Burney's Collection of Theatrical Portraits in the British Museum. Another is by G. Pulley (folio), dancing a hornpipe, with the song, and a third by Watson. Her life was published in 1760.

Oh, ne'er shall I forget the night,
　The stars were bright above me,
And gently lent their silv'ry light,
　When first she vow'd to love me.
But now I'm bound to Brighton camp,
　Kind Heaven, then, pray guide me,
And send me safely back again
　To the girl I've left behind me.

Had I the art to sing her praise
　With all the skill of Homer,
One only theme should fill my lays—
　The charms of my true lover.
So, let the night be e'er so dark,
　Or e'er so wet and windy,
Kind Heaven send me back again
　To the girl I've left behind me.

Her golden hair, in ringlets fair,
　Her eyes like diamonds shining,
Her slender waist, with carriage chaste,
　May leave the swan repining.
Ye gods above! oh, hear my prayer,
　To my beauteous fair to bind me,
And send me safely back again
　To the girl I've left behind me.

The bee shall honey taste no more,
　The dove become a ranger,
The falling waves shall cease to roar,
　Ere I shall seek to change her.
The vows we register'd above
　Shall ever cheer and bind me,
In constancy to her I love,—
　The girl I've left behind me.

This air is contained in a manuscript once in the possession of Dr. Rimbault, of date about 1770, and in several manuscript collections of military music of the latter half of the last century. It is a march, and is either entitled *The Girl I left behind me*, or *Brighton Camp*.

Although there were encampments along the coast between 1691 and

# THE LATER POPULAR MUSIC. 189

1693, before the victory of La Hogue, I do not attribute the song to so early a date, because I find no traces either of the words or music in the numerous publications in the first half of the eighteenth century; but in 1758 and 1759 there were also encampments, whilst Admirals Hawke and Rodney were watching the French fleet in Brest harbour. The French had prepared "flat-bottomed boats" for the landing of troops. In 1759, all danger of a descent upon our coast was averted by Admiral Boscawen's victory over one French fleet, and Admiral Hawke's over another. These and other successes of the year were chronicled in a song entitled "The year fifty-nine." In that year, also, a farce was printed, entitled *The Invasion*, to ridicule the unnecessary apprehensions which some persons had entertained of a nocturnal descent upon our coast by means of the flat-bottomed boats, and Garrick produced a pantomime, entitled *Harlequin's Invasion*, with the same object.

It appears, therefore, that the song of "The Girl I left behind me" may be dated, with great probability, in 1758.

In 1795, a song was written, entitled "Blyth Camps; or, The Girl I left behind me." It was printed in Bell's *Rhymes of the Northern Bards*, 8vo, Newcastle-upon-Tyne, 1812. It is a lame alteration of "Brighton Camp," commencing thus:—

> "I'm lonesome since I left Blyth camps,
> And *o'er* the moor that's *sedgy*,
> With heavy thoughts my mind is filled,
> Since I parted with my *Betsy*."

## HEART OF OAK.

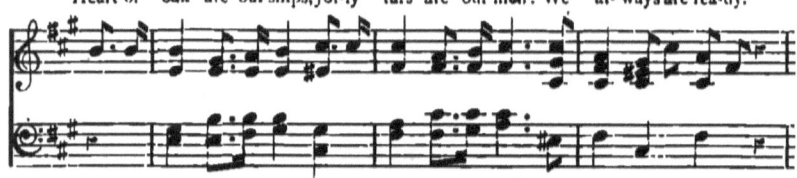

We ne'er see our foes but we wish them to stay;
They never see us but they wish us away:
If they run, why, we follow, and run them ashore,
For, if they won't fight us, what can we do more?
        Heart of oak, &c.

They swear they'll invade us, these terrible foes;
They frighten our women, our children, and beaux;
But, should their flat bottoms in darkness get o'er,
Still Britons they'll find to receive them on shore.
        Heart of oak, &c.

We'll still make them fear, and we'll still make them flee,
And drub 'em on shore, as we've drubb'd 'em at sea:
Then cheer up, my lads, with one heart let us sing,
Our soldiers, our sailors, our statesmen, our king.
        Heart of oak, &c.

We'll still make 'em run, and we'll still make 'em sweat,
In spite of the devil, and Brussels Gazette:
Then cheer up, my lads, with one heart let us sing,
Our soldiers, our sailors, our statesmen and king.
        Heart of oak, &c.

The words of this still popular song are by David Garrick, and it was sung by Mr. Champnes in *Harlequin's Invasion*, in 1759. The tune is by Dr. Boyce.

Many songs have been written to the air, and, among them, two in the Burney Collection. The first, " Keppel's Triumph," commencing :—

" Bear a hand, jolly tars, for bold Keppel appear,
In spite of each charge from Sir Hugh Palliser " :

the second, " The Hardy Tars of Old England ; or, The True Hearts of Oak," beginning :—

" Come, cheer up, my lads, let us haste to the main,
And rub out old scores with the dollars of Spain."

## RULE, BRITANNIA.

*The Judgment of Paris*, a Masque, by Dr. Arne.

192        THE LATER POPULAR MUSIC.

Although first printed by Dr. Arne, at the end of the masque of the *Judgment of Paris*, this song was composed for his masque of *Alfred*, and first performed at Cliefden House, near Maidenhead, on August 1, 1740.[1]

Dr. Arne afterwards altered this masque into an opera, and it was so performed at Drury Lane Theatre, on March 20, 1745, for the benefit of Mrs. Arne. In the advertisements of that performance, and in another of the following month, Dr. Arne entitles *Rule, Britannia* " a

---

[1] Cliefden was then the residence of Frederick, Prince of Wales, and the occasion was to commemorate the accession of George I., and in honour of the birthday of the young Princess Augusta.

*celebrated* ode"; from which it may be inferred that (although the entire masque had not been performed in public) *Rule, Britannia* had then attained popularity. Some detached pieces of the masque had been sung in Dublin, on the occasion of Arne's visit with his wife, but no record of any other public performance has hitherto been discovered.

The words of the masque were by Thomson and Mallet, but Thomson seems to have taken the lead in the affair, since, in the newspapers of the day, he alone is mentioned as the author. In the book, the names of Thomson and Mallet are both given.[1]

*Rule, Britannia* soon became a favourite with the Jacobite party. Ritson mentions a Jacobite parody, of which he was unable to procure a copy, but the chorus ran thus:—

"Rise, Britannia! Britannia, rise and fight!
Restore your injured monarch's right."

Another will be found in *The True Royalist; or, Chevalier's Favorite: being a collection of Elegant Songs never before printed*. It is entitled "A Song: tune, *When Britain first, at heav'n's command.*"

"Britannia, rouse at heav'n's command!
And crown thy native Prince again;
Then Peace shall bless thy happy land,
And Plenty pour in from the main:
Then shalt thou be—Britannia, thou shalt be—
From home and foreign tyrants free, &c.

This is followed by another, commencing:—

"When our great Prince, with his choice band,
Arriv'd from o'er the azure main,
Heav'n smil'd with pleasure, with pleasure on the land,
And guardian Angels sung this strain:
Go, brave hero; brave hero, boldly go,
And wrest thy sceptre from thy foe."

---

[1] The authorship of *Rule, Britannia* has been ascribed to Thomson, by Ritson, and other authorities, but a claim has recently been made for Mallet, on the strength of an advertisement prefixed by him to an altered edition of *Alfred*, in 1751, after Thomson's death. He writes thus:—"According to the present arrangement of the fable, I was obliged to reject a great deal of what I had written in the other; neither could I retain of my friend's part more than three or four single speeches and a part of one song." It appears, however, that three stanzas of *Rule, Britannia* were retained, and three others added by Lord Bolingbroke: such an argument in favour of Mallet is therefore very inconclusive. The only point in it is, that Mallet uses the word "song" in the advertisement, and retains the title of "ode" in the book; but *Rule, Britannia* may with equal accuracy be described as a song. Would Mallet have allowed Lord Bolingbroke so to mutilate the most successful song in the piece, if it had been his own? For internal evidence in favour of Thomson, see his poems, "Britannia" and "Liberty." Further information about *Rule, Britannia* will be found in Dr. Dinsdale's excellent edition of Mallet's works, and in the pages of *Notes and Queries*, including a refutation of M. Schœlcher's charge against Arne of having copied from Handel. See 2nd series, Nos. 86, 99, 103, 109, 111, and 120.

## GOD SAVE OUR LORD THE KING.

*Harmonia Anglicana,* 1742 (?).

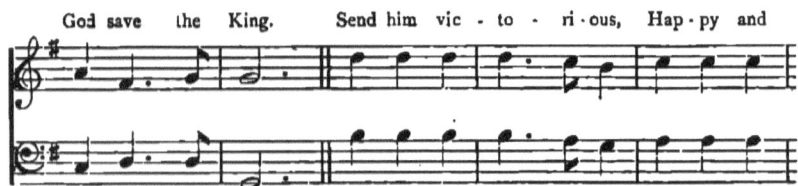

> O Lord our God, arise,
> Scatter his enemies,
>   And make them fall :
> Confound their politicks,
> Frustrate their knavish tricks,
> On him our hopes are fix'd,
>   O save us all.

The full title of the work from which the above version is taken is: "Harmonia Anglicana ; A Collection of two, three, and four-part songs; several of them never before printed. To which are added some Choice Dialogues, set to music by the most eminent masters, viz., Dr. Blow, H. Purcell, Handel, Dr. Green, Dl. Purcell, Eccles, Weldon, Leveridge, Lampe, Carey, &c. The whole revis'd, carefully corrected, and figur'd by a judicious master. London, Printed for, and sold by John Simpson, at the Bass Viol and Flute in Sweeting's Alley, opposite the East Door of the Royal Exchange." [1742 (?)[1]]

Before the discovery[2] of this version, the earliest known was that printed in *The Gentleman's Magazine* for October, 1745, which consists of the three stanzas which are still usually sung, and commences "God save great George our King." In the table of contents of *The Gentleman's Magazine* the older title of "God save our Lord the King" is retained; and when the *Harmonia Anglicana* was extended to two volumes, and the name changed to *Thesaurus Musicus*, although the song was then printed as "God save *great George* our King," the index remained unaltered—"God save our Lord the King."

[A version of the words somewhat different from either of these, and in Latin, is known to have been in existence about the same time:—

| | |
|---|---|
| O Deus optime, | Exurgat Dominus; |
| Salvum nunc facito | Rebelles dissipet, |
| Regem nostrum: | Et reprimat; |
| Sit laeta victoria | Dolos confundito; |
| Comes et gloria, | Fraudes depellito; |
| Salvum jam facito, | In te sit sita spes; |
| Tu Dominum. | O salva nos. |

These are the words of a "Latin Chorus," sung at a concert given by John Travers, of which the book of words exists. The date of the concert is unknown; but it must have been later than 1743,[3] and, from the special reference to rebels in the Chorus, may have been 1745. Many attempts have been made to throw back the date of the words, both Latin and English, into the previous century, but without success.

There is no record of the music to which the "Latin Chorus" was sung at Travers' concert, but it is difficult to avoid the conclusion that it must have been some arrangement either of the tune given above at the head, or of the slightly altered version first sung upon the stages of Drury Lane and Covent Garden Theatres in September, 1745, and during the rebellion.

---

[1] The *Harmonia Anglicana* is printed without date, but a clue to the time of publication is obtained in the following way. There are several works advertised by the publisher on the title-page, and three or four more seem to have been added subsequently to fill up vacant space on the index plate. The last of these are "Two collections of favourite Scotch tunes, set for a violin, German flute, or harpsichord, by Mr. Oswald." These two collections were advertised in November, 1742.

[2] By our author.—ED.]

[3] In the book of words an Ode on the Birthday of the Princess of Wales is said to have been "composed in the year 1743."

No question in the history of music has been more hotly debated than that which relates to the origin and authorship of this tune; and nothing, considering that it is composed entirely of very common phrases, is more surprising than the assurance with which theories based upon the imperfect resemblance of a few notes have been put forward, while the more weighty evidence afforded by the remarkable structure of the tune has been almost entirely overlooked.

The tune consists of two strains, of which the first has six measures, in groups of two, and the second eight, also in groups of two. This form is peculiar to a variety of the Galliard, a lively dance in triple measure, which, in the sixteenth century, always followed immediately upon the slow and stately Pavan. The classical form of the Galliard, consisting of two strains of eight measures each,[1] which was apparently the only form known before the year 1600, began, after that date, to give way to some extent to varieties, among which this of six and eight seems, if we may judge from the number of examples during the first quarter of the seventeenth century, to have been most in favour. Galliards in this form will be found in almost all the collections of lute and virginal music of the period. William Ballet's lute-book contains two, "A Galliard caled Phillida," and "Lost is my liberty"; in B.M. Addl. MSS. 30,485 is one by "Mr. Kinloughe," another by "Mr. Marchante," and another by "Mr. Byrde"; in Addl. MSS. 23,623, which consists entirely of organ and virginal music by Dr. John Bull, there are two; another, also by Bull, will be found in *Parthenia;* and so on. Towards the middle of the century the examples become rare, and long before the year 1700 the Galliard, in any form, was practically extinct.

These facts, which so far as I can see have hitherto escaped observation, appear to me to lend additional weight to the claim put forward by the late Mr. Richard Clark, of the Chapel Royal, in favour of a Galliard, (for such it really is) which he discovered in a MS. collection of virginal music by Dr. John Bull, transcribed about the year 1622.[2]

---

[1] Two fine examples of this form, *The Frog Galliard* and *Wigmore's Galliard*, are in the first volume of the present work. See pp. 274 and 250.

[2] It is not clear whether the title "Air" given to this piece in the published list of the contents of the MS. is a heading in the MS., or only a description by the maker of the list in default of a heading; for the list also contains—"page 77, Fantasia on a chromatic subject, a 4 v," and this is clearly given in place of a heading. But if the Galliard is called an Air in the MS., that does not exclude the other description. In a collection of Fantasias for strings and organ by John Jenkins, in the British Museum, pieces which are described as "Ayres" in the first violin part are called Galliards in all the others.

This Galliard, when it was exhibited by Mr. Clark to his friends, stood in the MS. as follows[1] :—

The resemblance here to the tune printed above at the head is extremely striking; indeed, I believe it would from the first have been admitted to be too close to be accidental, but for Mr. Clark's most unfortunate method of pursuing his researches.

---

[1] The MS. cannot now be seen, but a copy of this particular piece, made by Sir George Smart, is in existence, and was printed by Mr. W. H. Cummings in one of his excellent articles upon this subject in *The Musical Times*, March—Aug. 1878, from which I have taken it.

Our author says[1]:—"When Clark played the 'ayre' to me, with the book before him, I thought it to be the original of the national anthem; but afterwards, taking the manuscript into my own hands, I was convinced that it had been tampered with, and the resemblance strengthened, the sharps being in ink of a much darker colour than other parts. The additions are very perceptible, in spite of Clark's having covered the face of that portion with varnish.[2] In its original state, the 'ayre' commenced with these notes:—

 The *g* being natural, the resemblance to 'God save the King' does not strike the ear, but by making the *g* sharp, and changing the whole from an old scale without sharps or flats, into the modern scale of A major (three sharps), the tune becomes *essentially* like 'God save the King.' When I reflected further upon the matter, it appeared very improbable that Dr. Bull should have composed a piece for the organ in the modern key of A major. The most curious part of the resemblance between Dr. Bull's 'ayre' and 'God save the King' is that the first phrase consists of six bars, and the second of eight, which similarity does not exist in any other of the airs from which it is supposed to have been taken. It is true that the eight bars of the second phrase are made out by holding on[3] the final note of the melody through two bars, therefore it differs decidedly from all copies of our more modern tune; but the words may be sung to Dr. Bull's 'ayre' by dividing the time of the long notes—in fact, it has been so performed in public."

It would have been more satisfactory if our author had been able to tell us whether *all* the accidentals were in the different ink; though even if they were, it would only go to prove that Mr. Clark had blackened the existing accidentals to make them fall in with his added ones, for it is impossible that none of the sharps were intended by the composer. In the very example given by our author the G must have been originally sharp, and I am myself strongly of opinion that if the original

---

[1] In the previous edition of this work.

[2] Mr. Clark bought the MS. in the hope of proving that a composition contained in it at fol. 56, called *God save the King*, was the original of the national anthem. Although that composition turned out to be totally unlike it, he discovered, by a most extraordinary coincidence, at fol. 98, this Galliard which resembles it so closely. It would seem that, not content with this discovery, and with the insertion of some sharps, more or less, he also wrote something in the MS., which might make it appear that the composition at fol. 98 was the *second part* of that at fol. 56.

[3] It would be more correct to say "expanding the final note."

MS. should ever be seen again, it will be found that the greater number of the chromatic signs here printed, especially in the second strain, are genuine. The first quarter of the seventeenth century was the age of chromatic experiments. The key system had not yet been reached, but the modes were breaking down; and a favourite experiment (especially with Bull), in the smaller sportive pieces for instruments, was the introduction of the major third in a mode where it is by nature minor.[1] But even if every chromatic sign were removed from this composition, the continuous resemblance merely in the position of the notes would still be sufficient, I should think, to establish its identity with the later one.

The treatment of the last two bars in the Galliard, to which our author refers, was very common in the instrumental music of the period, especially in settings of known tunes.[2] And seeing that the plagal cadence which here follows the authentic one is included within the eight measures of the second strain, Bull's composition may possibly be a setting of something more or less well known at the time. Should this be so, a diligent search among the existing lute and virginal music of this period would be almost certain to reveal it.

We have no sure means of tracing the connection between this Galliard of Bull's and the tune in *Harmonia Anglicana*. But as it is known that Henry Carey, a contributor to *Harmonia Anglicana*, asked the help of a more experienced musician—John Christopher Smith, Handel's amanuensis—in setting a bass to the tune, we may suppose it was through him. The MS. containing the Galliard was at that time in London, in the library of Dr. Pepusch, and there is nothing impossible in the supposition that Carey may have seen it, or perhaps some other copy or version, if not this. The fact that Carey's claim to the tune was made not by himself, but by his son,[3] has sometimes been

---

[1] See vol. i. of the present work, p. 69. And one of the Galliards by Bull in Addl. MS., 23,623, referred to above, which is written in the Dorian Mode, has the natural minor third made major throughout the piece, almost without exception.

[2] See vol. i., p. 110.

[3] Mr. G. S. Carey received the following letter from Dr. Harington, of Bath, dated June 13, 1795:—

"DEAR SIR,—The anecdote you mention, respecting your father's being the author and composer of the words and music of 'God save the King,' is certainly true. That most respectable gentleman, my worthy friend and patient, Mr. Smith, has often told me what follows: viz., 'that your father came to him with the words and music, desiring him to correct the bass, which was not proper; and, at your father's request, Mr. Smith wrote another bass in correct harmony.' Mr. Smith, to whom I read your letter this day, repeated the same account, and on his authority I pledge myself for the truth of the statement.

"H. HARINGTON."

considered fatal to the notion of his connection with it in any way. But since comparison with the Galliard shews clearly how little of it could have been his own, his reticence was not very surprising ; and as he died the year after the publication of *Harmonia Anglicana*, and two years before the rebellion of 1745, which made the tune popular, he had, apparently, but little either of opportunity or temptation to break silence.—ED.]

# APPENDIX.

# ANGLO-SCOTTISH SONGS.

BEFORE closing this book, it may be desirable to devote a short space to the subject of the English and Anglo-Scottish songs and tunes which are incorporated in collections of Scottish music. Those who have not inquired into the subject may not be aware that many of the songs of Allan Ramsay, Burns, and other Scotch poets, were written to English tunes, and that those tunes, being now known by the names of their songs, pass with the world for Scotch.

Ritson tells us, in his *Historical Essay on Scotch Song*, that "the vulgar language of the lowland Scots was always called English by their own writers till a late period," and that "the vulgar toung in Scottis" meant Gaelic or Erse. The quotations he adduces carry the proof down to the first half of the sixteenth century; but, in the early part of the eighteenth, this use of the word "English" was altogether dropped, and "Scots Sangs" included not only songs written by Scotchmen, whether in the lowland dialect or in English, but also the meaning was extended to any purely English songs that were popular in Scotland. As the works of Scotch poets are now sometimes included under the head of English literature, where the preponderance is English, so Allan Ramsay entitled his *Tea Table Miscellany* "a collection of Scots Sangs," the preponderance in the two first volumes (of which the work originally consisted) being Scotch. Although it was soon extended to three volumes, and the third was entirely English, still the exclusive title of "Scots Sangs" was retained. In 1740 a fourth was added, partly consisting of Scotch and partly of English. In this are twenty-one songs by Gay, from *The Beggars' Opera*, ranged consecutively.

It would have been a great assistance to after-inquiry if Ramsay had confined his selection to songs by Scotch authors, instead of thus mixing up those of the two countries; and it would have been more easy to separate the respective tunes if he had in all cases given the names by which they were previously known. How far this was required to divide the English from the Scotch will be best exemplified by supplying the names of the tunes to half a dozen of Ramsay's own songs.

"My mither's ay glowrin o'er me," to the country dance of *A Health to Betty;* "The maltman comes on Monday," to the tune of *Roger de Coverley;* "Peggy, I must love thee," to the tune of *The Deel assist the plotting Whigs*,[1] composed by Purcell; "The bonny grey-ey'd morn begins to peep," to the tune of "an excellent new Play-house song, call'd *The bonny grey-ey'd morn*, or *Jockey rous'd with love*," composed by Jeremiah Clark; "Corn riggs are bonny," to the tune of *Sawney was tall and of noble race*, a song in D'Urfey's play, *The Virtuous Wife;* "Nanny O," to the tune of the English ballad of *Nanny O*.[2]

If this kind of scrutiny were carried through the songs in the *Tea Table Miscellany*, in Thomson's *Orpheus Caledonius*, or any other collection, the bulk of Scottish music would be sensibly diminished; but, on the whole, it would gain in symmetry. Many good and popular tunes would be given up, but a mass of indifferent would be rejected at the same time

The mixture of English and Anglo-Scottish with the genuine Scottish music has been gradually increasing since Thomson's time. Successive collectors have added songs that were popular in their day, without care as to the source whence they were derived; each seeking only to render his own publication more attractive than those of his predecessors. The songs of English musicians—often of living authors—have been thus included, and their names systematically suppressed. Although the authorship of these songs may have been known to many at the time of publication, it soon passed out of memory, and the Scotch have themselves been deceived into a belief in their genuineness. Thus Burns, writing to Mr. Candlish, in June, 1787, about Johnson's *Scots Musical*

---

[1] "The Deel assist the plotting Whigs" is the first line of "The Whigs' Lamentable Condition; or, The Royalists' Resolution: to *a pleasant new tune*." The words and music are contained in 180 *Loyal Songs*, 1685 and 1694, and the music alone in *Musick's Handmaid*, Part II., 1689, as "a Scotch tune," composed by Purcell. In *Pills to purge Melancholy*, Vol. I., 1699 to 1714, the song of "Tom and Will were Shepherd Swains" is adapted to the air.

[2] This ballad and the answer to it are in the Roxburghe Collection. The first (ii. 415) is "The Scotch wooing of Willy and Nanny: to *a pleasant new tune, or Nanny, O*."

Printed by P. Brooksby. Although entitled "The *Scotch* wooing," it relates to the most southern part of Northumberland. It commences, "As I went forth one morning fair," and has for burden—

"It is Nanny, Nanny, Nanny O,
  The love I bear to Nanny O,
All the world shall never know
  The love I bear to Nanny O."

Tynemouth Castle is spelled "Tinmouth" in the ballad, just as it is now pronounced in the North of England; it is, therefore, probably, of Northumbrian origin. The answer is in Rox. ii. 17; also printed by Brooksby.

*Museum*, says :—" I am engaged in assisting an honest Scotch enthusiast, a friend of mine, who is an engraver, and has taken it into his head to publish a collection of all our songs set to music, of which the words and music are done by Scotsmen." And again, in October, to another correspondent :—" An engraver, James Johnson, in Edinburgh, has, not from mercenary views, but from an honest Scotch enthusiasm, set about collecting *all our native songs*," &c. And yet, within the first twenty-four songs of the only volume then published, are compositions by Purcell, Michael Arne, Hook, Berg, and Battishill.

Thomson's *Orpheus Caledonius* was printed in London ; but the *Scots Musical Museum* was published in Edinburgh.

Although the popularity of Scottish music in England cannot be dated further back than the reign of Charles II.,[1] it may be proved, from various sources, that English music was in favour in Scotland from the fifteenth century, and that many English airs became so popular as at length to be thoroughly domiciled there. The *Extracts from the Accounts of the Lords High Treasurers of Scotland* from the year 1474 to 1642, printed by Mr. Dauney, shew that there were English harpers, lutenists, pipers, and pipers with the drone, or bagpipers, among the musicians at the Scottish Court, besides others under the general name of English minstrels. Among the sweet songs said to be sung by the shepherds in Wedderburn's *Complainte of Scotlande*, 1549, are several English still extant (one composed by Henry VIII. taking precedence on the list) ; and the religious parodies, such as in *Ane Compendious Booke of Godly and Spirituall Songs*, are commonly upon English songs and ballads. English tunes have hitherto been found in every Scottish manuscript that contains any Scotch airs, if written before 1730. There is, I believe, no exception to this rule,—at least I may cite all those I have seen, and the well-authenticated transcripts of others. They include Wood's manuscripts ; the Straloch, the Rowallan, and the Skene MSS. ; Dr. Leyden's Lyra-Viol Book, the MSS. that were in the possession of the late Andrew Blaikie; Mrs. Agnes Hume's book, and others in the Advocates' Library ; those in the possession of Mr. David

---

[1] It is difficult to account wholly for this, but it may be attributed partially to the prejudice against the Scotch, who were longed viewed as interlopers, and somewhat to their broad dialect; for, although they would naturally sing the airs of their country, I cannot find that any attained popularity in England before the Restoration, either by notices of dramatists and other writers, by being used as ballad tunes, or by being found in print or manuscript. I should say that one or two airs are the most that could be adduced. The upper classes of both countries seem to have sung only scholastic music, and the lower order of English had abundant ballad tunes of their own, and were apparently loth to change them.

Laing, and many of minor note. Some of the Scotch manuscripts contain English music exclusively. I have recently analyzed the contents of Hogg's *Jacobite Relics of Scotland*, and find half the songs in the first volume to have been derived from English printed collections, but if the modern were taken away and only the old suffered to remain, the proportion would be much larger. As Hogg took these songs from Scotch manuscripts, his book shews the extent to which the words of old English songs are still stored in Scotland. The appendix of Jacobite songs and those of the Whigs at the end of the volume are almost exclusively from these collections.

Before the publication of Ramsay's *Tea Table Miscellany*, the "Scotch tunes" that were popular in England were mostly spurious, and the words adapted to them seem to have been invariably so. Of this I could give many instances, but it may suffice to quote one from *A Second Tale of a Tub*, which, being printed in 1715, is within nine years of Ramsay's publication. "Each party call for particular tunes . . . the blue bonnets" (*i.e.*, the Scotch) "had very good voices, but being at the furthest end of the room, were not distinctly heard. Yet they split their throats in hollowing out *Bonny Dundee, Valiant Jockey, Sawney was a dawdy lad,* [bonny lad ?] and *'Twas within a furlong of Edinborough town.*"

*Bonnie Dundee* commences thus :—

"Where gott'st thou the haver-meal bannock? [oatmeal cake]
Blind booby, canst thou not see?
Ise got it out of the Scotchman's wallet," &c.

The subject of the ballad is "Jockey's Escape from Dundee," and it ends, "Adieu to bonny Dundee," from which the tune takes the title of *Adew Dundie* in the Skene manuscript, and of *Bonny Dundee* in *The Dancing Master*. It first appeared in the latter publication in a second appendix to the addition of 1686, printed in 1688. "Valiant Jockey's march'd away," and "'Twas within a furlong of Edinborough town," are by D'Urfey; and "Sawney was a *bonny* lad"[1] by P. A. Motteux, the tune by Purcell.

Songs in imitation of the Scottish dialect seem to have been confined to the stage till about the years 1679 and 1680,[2] when the Duke of York,

---

[1] If not this, it must be "*Jockey* was a dawdy lad," a Scotch song by D'Urfey in *The Campaigners*. There is a Sawney in that song, but he is the favoured lover. The music was composed and sung by Mr. Wilkins.

[2] I do not include songs like "Sing, home again, Jockey," (upon the defeat of the Scottish army,) or others written *against* the Scotch, which may contain a few words in imitation of the dialect.

afterwards James II., was sent to govern Scotland, pending the discussion on the Exclusion Bill in the Houses of Parliament. The Whigs were endeavouring to debar him from succession to the throne, as being a Roman Catholic, while the most influential Scotch and English loyalists, then newly named Tories, were as warmly espousing his cause.

Among the ballad-writers, the royalists greatly preponderated, and the Scotch were in especial favour with them. Mat. Taubman, the city of London pageant-writer, was one of these loyal poets. He published many songs in the Duke's favour, which he afterwards collected into a volume, with "An Heroic Poem," on his return from Scotland. Nat. Thompson, the printer, collected and published 120 *Loyal Songs*, which he subsequently enlarged to 180. Besides these, there are songs extant on broadsides, with music, which are not included in any collection. Occasional attempts at the Scottish dialect are to be found in all these sources. Purcell, and other musicians in the service of the Court, readily set such songs to music; indeed, from the time of the Exclusion Bill until he became king, James seems to have had all the song-writers in his favour.

Perhaps the earliest extant specimen of a ballad printed in Scotland may also be referred to this period:—I mean by "ballad" that which was intended to be sung, and not poetry printed on broadsides, without the name of the tune, even though such may sometimes have been called "ballets." Of the latter we have specimens by Robert Sempill, or Semple, printed in Edinburgh as early as 1570; but, as a real ballad, intended to be sung about the country, as English ballads were, I know none earlier than "The Banishment of Poverty, by his R. H., J. D. A. [James, Duke of Albany], to the tune of the *Last Good Night*." It is to be observed that this is to an English tune, and so are many of the ballads that were printed in Scotland, some being reprints of those published in London. Among others in the possession of Mr. David Laing are "A proper new Ballad intituled The Gallant Grahames: to its own proper tune, *I will away and will not stay*." This is a white-letter reprint of "An excellent new ballad entituled The Gallant Grahams *of Scotland*," a copy of which is in the Roxburghe Collection, iii. 380, to the same tune. "Bothwell Banks is bonny; or, A Description of the new Mylne of Bothwell," is to the English tune of *Who can blame my woe*. "The Life and Bloody Death of Mrs. Laurie's Dog" is "to the tune *The Ladies Daughter*" [of Paris properly].—(See Evans's *Old Ballads*.) The above are on Scottish subjects, but there are also reprints of the Anglo-Scottish, such as "Blythe Jockie, young and gay," (the tune of which is by Leveridge,) and "Valiant Jockey's march'd away," before mentioned;

as well as of purely English ballads, like "Room, room for a Rover; or, An innocent Country Life prefer'd before the noisy clamours of a restless town. To *a new tune*":—

"Room, room for a rover,
London is so hot," &c.

The mixture of English music in Scotch collections is not without inconvenience to the Scots themselves, for an essayist who intends to write about Scottish music must either be content to deal in generalities, or he will be liable to the mistake of praising English music where he intends to praise Scotch. Dr. Beattie, in one of his published letters, says of the celebrated Mrs. Siddons, "She loves music, and is fond of Scotch tunes, many of which I played to her on the violoncello. One of these, *She rose and let me in*, which you know is a favourite of mine, made the tears start from her eyes. 'Go on,' said she, 'and you will soon have your revenge;' meaning that I should draw as many tears from her as she had drawn from me" by her acting.—(*Life of James Beattie, LL.D.*, by Sir W. Forbes, ii. 139.) Dr. Beattie was evidently not aware that both the music and words of *She rose and let me in* are English.

It is not only by essayists that mistakes are made, for even in historical works like "Ancient Scottish Melodies from a Manuscript of the reign of James VI., with an introductory enquiry illustrative of the History of the Music of Scotland, by William Dauney, F.S.A., Scot.," airs which bear no kind of resemblance to Scottish music are claimed as Scotch. Mr. Dauney seems to have been a firm believer in the authenticity of the collections of Scottish music, and to have thought the evidence of an air being found in a Scotch manuscript sufficient to prove its Scottish origin. In such cases dates were to him of minor importance. Thus, *Franklin is fled away; When the King enjoys his own again; I pray you, love, turn to me; Macbeth; The Nightingale; The Milking-pail; Philporter's Lament*, and many others, are set down as airs of "which Scotland may claim the parentage." As to the Anglo-Scottish and English Northern songs, at the very opening of his book Mr. Dauney claims five in *Pills to purge Melancholy*, without noticing Ritson's counter-statement as to two (yet appropriating them under those names), or that a third was stated to be a country-dance tune in the book he quotes. This is indeed driving over obstacles.

The manuscripts from which the "Ancient Scottish Melodies" are derived are known as the Skene Manuscripts, from having been in the possession of the family of that name. They consist of seven small books of lute music of uniform size, and are now bound in one. Mr. Dauney admits that a portion of the airs are English, but follows the Ramsay precedent in the title of his book. I have recently examined these manuscripts with some care,[1] and am decidedly of opinion, both from the writing and from the airs they contain, that they are not, and cannot be, of the reign of James VI. James VI. of Scotland and I. of England died in 1625.

As to the sixth manuscript, which Mr. Dauney considers to be "evidently the oldest of all," the first fourteen airs in the fifth, and the whole of the sixth, are, in my opinion, in the same handwriting. The music is there written in the lozenge-shaped note, which is nowhere else employed. Among the airs in the fifth, we find *Adieu, Dundee*, which was not included in *The Dancing Master* before the appendix of 1688; and *Three Sheep-skins*, an English country-dance (*not* a ballad tune), which first appeared in *The Dancing Master* of 1698.

I leave it to Scottish antiquaries to determine whether corroborative evidence of the date of the manuscripts may not be found among the titles of their own airs. Mr. Dauney even passed over *Leslei's Lilt* without a suspicion that it derived its name from the Scotch general in the civil wars. A march[2] and another air were certainly named after him before the Restoration.

---

[1] My attention has recently been drawn to these manuscripts, which I had not seen for twenty years, from finding, in the course of my attempts at chronological arrangement, that their supposed date could not be reconciled with other evidence. I have hitherto quoted the Skene MSS as about 1630 or 1640, many of the airs they contain are undoubtedly of that date—some, like those of Dowland and the masque tunes of James I., unquestionably earlier. In Mr. Dauney's book the airs are not published in the order in which they are found in the manuscripts, and some airs (besides duplicates) are omitted. The printed index is not very correct—for instance, "Let never crueltie dishonour beauty" is not included in it. The earliest writing appears to be "Lady, wilt thou love me?" at the commencement of Part II. ; but all the remainder of that part seems to be a century later. Pages 62 to 80 are blank. At the end of the first manuscript are the words "Finis quod Skine," which Mr. Dauney considers to be the writing of John Skene, who died in 1644. Independently of other evidence, the large number of duplicates would show the improbability of the collection having been made for one person. For instance, "Horreis Galziard" is contained in Parts I. and III.— "I left my love behind me,"in Parts II. and III. —"My Lady Laukian's Lilt," "Scerdustis," "Scullione," and "Pitt on your shirt on Monday," in Parts III. and V.—"My Lady Rothemais Lilt,"in Parts III. and VI.—"Blew Breiks," in Parts III. and VII.—"I love my love for love again," in Parts V. and VI.

This is not the only manuscript, English or Scotch, the age of which I now find reason to doubt. Among the Scotch, that of Mr. Andrew Blaikie, said to bear a date of 1692, (which I by no means deny, although I did not observe it in the book when lent to me,) cannot have been written before 1745. It contains "God save the King," and other airs not to be reconciled with the usually attributed date.

[2] I do not mean the tune which Oswald prints in the second volume of his *Caledonian Pocket Companion* under the name of *Lasly's March*, but the *Lesleyes March* in Playford's *Musick's Recreation on the Lyra Viol*, 1656.

P

It is curious to mark the difference between English and Scotch writers on the music of their respective countries; Dr. Burney, like the fashionable Englishman, minutely chronicling the Italian operas of his day, and hesitating not to misquote Hall, Hollinshed, and Hentzner, to get rid of the trouble of writing about the music of England; and the Scotch sturdily maintaining the credit of Scotland—some being intent rather upon putting forth fresh claims than too nicely scrutinizing those already advanced, if they tell in favour of their country.

It is time, however, that we should have one collection to consist exclusively of Scottish music. Burns and George Thomson confess in their published correspondence to having taken any Irish airs that suited them, and even in Wood's *Songs of Scotland* the publisher's plan has been to include all the best and most popular airs, and not to limit the selection to such as are strictly of Scottish origin.

The separation of the English and Irish tunes from the Scotch in these collections was nominally attempted by Mr. Stenhouse in his notes upon airs in Johnson's *Scots Musical Museum*. I say "nominally," for his notes are like historical novels,—wherever facts do not chime in with the plan of the tale, imagination supplies the deficiencies. Mr. Stenhouse's plan was threefold,—firstly, to claim as Scotch every good tune that had become popular in Scotland; secondly, to prove that every song of doubtful or disputed parentage came to England from Scotland "at the union of the two crowns"; and, thirdly, to supply antiquity to such Scotch airs as required it. All this he accomplished in a way quite peculiar to himself. Invention supplied authors and dates, and fancy inscribed the tunes in sundry old manuscripts, where the chances were greatly against any one's searching to find them. If the search should be made, will it not be made by Scotchmen? Englishmen care only for foreign music, and do not trouble themselves about the matter; and will Scotchmen expose what has been done from such patriotic motives? Upon no other ground than this imaginary impunity can I account for the boldness of Mr. Stenhouse's inventions.

Unfortunately for his fame, two of his own countrymen did not think all this ingenuity necessary for the reputation of Scottish music. Mr. David Laing, therefore, made a tolerably clear sweep of his dates, and Mr. George Farquhar Graham of his quotations from old musical manuscripts. The former supposed Mr. Stenhouse "mistaken," "deceived"; the variety of his accomplishments was not to be discovered at once.

The second occasionally administered rebuke in more explicit language; but to the present day the depths of Stenhouse's invention have not been half fathomed.

Some of the effects of his ingenuity will never be wholly obviated. One class of inventions is very difficult to disprove, where he fixes upon an author for a song, or makes a tale of the circumstances under which it was written. Such evidence, as in the case of *She rose and let me in*, will not always be at hand to refute him, and much of this class of fiction still remains for those who are content to quote from so imaginative a source.

It is to be hoped that any who may henceforth quote from him will give their authority, for he has sometimes been copied without acknowledgment, and thus his fictions have been endorsed by respectable names.[1]

---

[1] Although Dauney's *Ancient Scottish Melodies* were printed in 1838, and Stenhouse's *Notes* issued in 1839 (after having been kept for many years in Messrs. Blackwood's cellars), it is evident that Dauney had access to, and was one of those led into error by them. As an instance, at p. 17, he says: "It was in the year 1680 when the Scottish air, *Katherine Ogie*, was sung by Mr. Abell, a gentleman of the Chapel Royal, at his concert in Stationers' Hall." The date of 1680 is purely Stenhousian, and can only have been copied from the following characteristic specimen of the *Notes*:—"This fine old *Scottish* song, beginning, 'As I went furth to view the plain,' was introduced and sung by Mr. John Abell, a gentleman of the Chapel Royal, at his concert in Stationers' Hall, London, *in the year* 1680, *with great applause.* It was also printed with the music and words, by an engraver of the name of Cross, as a single-sheet song, *in the course of that year, a copy of which is now lying before me.*" In the first place, Cross did not engrave in 1680, and the single-sheet song, "Bonny Kathern Oggy, as it was sung by Mr. Abell at his concert in Stationers' Hall," bears no date. Abell was a gentleman of the Chapel Royal during the latter part of the reign of Charles II., and the whole of that of James II. Having turned Papist when James became King, he quitted England at the Revolution of 1688, but was permitted to return by William III. towards the close of the year 1700. From *that* time, being without any fixed employment, and having acquired great repute as a singer, he occasionally gave public concerts, the first of which I find any announcement having taken place at Covent Garden on the 29th Dec., 1702. Stenhouse, to make his story complete, tells us that Abell died "about the year 1702," although Hawkins (from whom he was copying so much of the story as suited his purpose) says that "about the latter end of *Queen Anne's reign*, Abell was at Cambridge with his lute."

Now, why all this invention? It was to get rid of the fact that the earliest known copy of the tune is in the Appendix to *The Dancing Master* of 1686, under the title of "*Lady Catherine Ogle,* a new Dance." D'Urfey wrote the first song to it, "Bonny Kathern Loggy," commencing, "As I came down the Highland town." This is contained in the *Pills* and in *The Merry Musician; or, A Cure for the Spleen,* i. 224, 1716. The latter publication includes also the "New song, to the tune of *Katherine Loggy,*" commencing, "As I walk'd forth to view the plain," i. 295, which Ramsay, after making some alterations, printed in the *Tea Table Miscellany.* The following is the first stanza of what Stenhouse terms the "fine old *Scottish* song," sung by Abell:—

"As I went forth to view the spring,
  Upon a morning early,
With May's sweet scent to chear my brain,
  When flowers grew fresh and fairly;
A vary pratty maid I spy'd,
  Sha shin'd tho' it was foggy,
I ask'd her name, Sweet sir, sha said,
  My name is Kathern Oggy."

It is a pleasure to turn from such an annotator to the editor of Wood's *Songs of Scotland;* for, besides exposing a great number of Stenhouse's mistatings, he has given judgment with strict impartiality wherever he felt called upon to exercise it in cases of disputed nationality. It is only to be regretted that Mr. Graham's opinion upon the internal evidence of airs was not more frequently expressed, and that any portion of Stenhouse's imaginative notes should have been incorporated in the work. Sometimes it is difficult to distinguish between what is on the authority of Mr. Graham and what of Stenhouse without having a copy of his notes by our side, but all I have had occasion to controvert *originated* with the latter.

END OF THE SECOND VOLUME.

# INDEX.

# INDEX.

| | PAGE |
|---|---|
| A-begging we will go | 42 |
| A damsel I'm told | 149 |
| Admiral Benbow | 92 |
| A-hunting we will go | 175 |
| All in the Downs | 144 |
| Amarillis | 12 |
| An old woman clothed in gray | 120 |
| An old woman poor and blind | 82 |
| As down in the meadows | 127 |
| At Winchester was a wedding | 49 |
| Ay, marry, and thank ye too | 70 |
| | |
| Bartholomew Fair | 77 |
| Benbow the brother tar | 94 |
| Black-ey'd Susan | 144 |
| Bonny bonny bird | 149 |
| Bonny Nell | 23 |
| Brave boys | 149 |
| Brighton Camp | 187 |
| | |
| Care, thou canker of our joys | 184 |
| Cavalilly man | 26 |
| Cease, rude Boreas | 166 |
| Cease your funning | 119 |
| Charles of Sweden | 109 |
| Cheshire Rounds | 167 |
| Chester waits | 11 |
| Cock Lorrel | 40 |

# INDEX.

| | PAGE |
|---|---|
| Colchester waits | 12 |
| Come jolly Bacchus | 109 |
| Come lasses and lads | 114 |
| Come, let us drink about | 180 |
| Come let us prepare | 105 |
| Come, open the door, sweet Betty | 147 |
| Come sweet lass | 73 |
| Courtiers, courtiers | 60 |
| Cupid's courtesie | 99 |
| Cupid's trepan | 149 |
| | |
| Death and the lady | 170 |
| Down among the dead men | 173 |
| | |
| Excuse me | 1 |
| | |
| Fair Margaret and sweet William | 131 |
| Fair Rosalind | 131 |
| Farewell, Manchester | 91 |
| Felton's Gavot | 91 |
| Franklin is fled away | 20 |
| | |
| God save our lord the King | 194 |
| Good morrow, gossip Joan | 98 |
| Greenwich Park | 73 |
| Grim king of the ghosts | 129 |
| | |
| Heart of oak | 189 |
| Here's a health to all honest men | 107 |
| Here's a health unto his Majesty | 18 |
| Hey ho, my honey | 14 |
| How stands the glass around | 134 |
| Humours of the Bath | 177 |
| | |
| I am a poor shepherd undone | 14 |
| I am so deep in love | 99 |
| I have but a mark a year | 86 |
| I have left the world as the world found me | 149 |
| I'll tell thee, Dick, where I have been | 43 |

# INDEX.

|  | PAGE |
|---|---|
| In January last | 30 |
| I often for my Jenny strove | 61 |
| I prethee, love, turn to me | 137 |
| | |
| Jamaica | 3 |
| James the Second's March | 65 |
| Joan's placket is torn | 57 |
| Joan to the maypole | 100 |
| | |
| Ladies of London | 64 |
| Law lies a-bleeding | 5 |
| Lay the bent to the bonny broom | 80 |
| Leather apron | 53 |
| Let Oliver now be forgotten | 121 |
| Lilliburlero | 58 |
| London is a fine town | 6 |
| London waits | 10 |
| Lord Frog | 22 |
| Lovely Nancy | 162 |
| | |
| Mad Moll | 74 |
| Mad Robin | 56 |
| May fair | 113 |
| May hill | 52 |
| Miss Dawson's hornpipe | 186 |
| Molly's hoop | 178 |
| My lodging it is on the cold ground | 140 |
| | |
| Nancy Dawson | 186 |
| | |
| O, good ale, thou art my darling | 179 |
| Oh, how they frisk it | 53 |
| O Jenny, Jenny, where hast thou been | 113 |
| Old Hewson the cobbler | 163 |
| Old Hob | 111 |
| Old King Cole | 171 |
| Old Noll's Jig | 87 |
| On the cold ground | 137 |
| On yonder high mountains | 136 |

# INDEX.

| | PAGE |
|---|---|
| Phillida flouts me | 133 |
| Phillis on the new-made hay | 13 |
| Poor Robin's Maggot | 116 |
| Portsmouth | 88 |
| Pretty Bessie | 17 |
| Pretty Polly Oliver | 181 |
| | |
| Red Bull | 71 |
| Roger of Coverly | 45 |
| Rule, Britannia | 191 |
| | |
| St. George for England | 102 |
| Sally in our alley | 117 |
| Shackley Hay | 83 |
| Shropshire Rounds | 168 |
| Sir Guy | 156 |
| Smiling Polly | 185 |
| Sweet Nelly my heart's delight | 125 |
| Sweet William's farewell | 144 |
| | |
| Taunton Dean | 158 |
| The baffled knight | 69 |
| The bailiff's daughter | 159 |
| The Barking barber | 183 |
| The blind beggar of Bethnal Green | 16 |
| The budgeon it is a delicate trade | 124 |
| The buff coat has no fellow | 1 |
| The button'd smock | 7 |
| The clear cavalier | 32 |
| The cobbler's hornpipe | 80 |
| The country courtship | 128 |
| The country garden | 122 |
| The delights of the bottle | 28 |
| The devil's progress | 75 |
| The dominion of the sword | 5 |
| The doubting virgin | 150 |
| The Duke of Berwick's March | 134 |
| The dusty miller | 166 |
| The Dutchwoman's Jigg | 77 |

# INDEX.

| | PAGE |
|---|---|
| The fading | 104 |
| The fair one let me in | 34 |
| The fit's upon me now | 27 |
| The garter | 65 |
| The girl I've left behind me | 187 |
| The happy clown | 108 |
| The jovial beggars | 52 |
| The jovial crew | 52 |
| The keel row | 185 |
| The King's Jig | 49 |
| The King of Poland | 60 |
| The lass of Cumberland | 24 |
| The leather bottle | 141 |
| The man of Kent | 112 |
| The mousetrap | 111 |
| The new Royal Exchange | 8 |
| The northern lass | 21 |
| The Northumberland bagpipes | 66 |
| The Oxfordshire tragedy | 153 |
| The Restoration of King Charles | 52 |
| The roast-beef of old England | 95 |
| The sailor's complaint | 165 |
| The Spanish lady | 84 |
| The spring's a-coming | 177 |
| The twenty-ninth of May | 52 |
| The Twitcher | 149 |
| The vicar of Bray | 122 |
| The virgin Queen | 74 |
| The women all tell me | 182 |
| There lives a lass upon the green | 160 |
| There was an old fellow at Waltham Cross | 158 |
| There was an old woman liv'd under a hill | 79 |
| There was a pretty lass and a tenant of my own | 169 |
| Thomas, you cannot | 17 |
| Three merry men of Kent | 161 |
| Three travellers | 97 |
| To all you ladies now at land | 154 |
| Tobacco's but an Indian weed | 78 |
| Tom Nokes' Jig | 148 |
| Turn again, Whittington | 89 |

## INDEX.

| | PAGE |
|---|---|
| Watton town's end ... ... ... ... ... | 6 |
| Was ever man so tost in love ... ... ... ... | 157 |
| When busy fame ... ... ... ... ... | 39 |
| When the stormy winds do blow ... ... ... | 47 |
| Why, soldiers, why ... ... ... ... ... | 134 |
| Willy was so blithe a lad ... ... ... ... | 68 |
| Woman's work is never done ... ... ... ... | 150 |
| | |
| Yellow stockings ... ... ... | 74 |
| You gentlemen of England ... ... | 47 |
| Young Jemmy ... ... ... ... | 36 |

www.ingramcontent.com/pod-product-compliance
Lightning Source LLC
Chambersburg PA
CBHW021824230426
43669CB00008B/856